The Great
Classic Yacht
Revival

The Great
Classic Yacht
Revival

Nic Compton
Foreword by Olin Stephens

RIZZOLI
NEW YORK

The Great Classic Yacht Revival
by **Nic Compton**

First published in the United States of America
in 2004 by Rizzoli International Publications, Inc.
300 Park Avenue South
New York, NY 10010
www.rizzoliusa.com

Originally published in Great Britain in 2004 by
Mitchell Beazley, an imprint of Octopus
Publishing Group Limited,
2–4 Heron Quays, London E14 4JP.
© Octopus Publishing Group Limited 2004
Text © Nic Compton 2004

Full credit to be given for all picture usage ie Nic
Compton/Salty Dog Media

ISBN 0-8478-2675-9

Library of Congress Control Number 2004093336

Commission Editor **Vivien Antwi**
Executive Art Editor **Christine Keilty**
Project Editor **Naomi Waters**
Design **Colin Goody**
Production **Gary Hayes**
Copy Editors **Adrian Morgan and Rona Johnson**
Proofreader **Charlie Eltham**
Indexer **Catherine Hall**

Set in Palatino Light

Printed and bound in China

contents

above It's all in the details. A brass stern light on the Abeking & Rasmussen ketch *Sintra* adds a touch of authenticity, which her famous German builders would appreciate.

foreword

As an interested participant I have been fascinated to read Nic Compton's account of the worldwide activity in restoring and sailing classic yachts. A long life has allowed me to live through most of the time span covered within these pages. I remember how, as a boy in America, I followed, excited, Sir Thomas Lipton's 1920 America's Cup challenge against *Resolute*. I became an omnivorous reader of yachting magazines and books like Dr. Worth's *Yacht Cruising*. Family sailing in small boats led to 1928 when I sailed offshore in the Bermuda Race with John Alden in his schooner, *Malabar IX*. His designs are now classics. We soon became colleagues and competitors.

In 1929, with Drake Sparkman as a partner, I started working at yacht design and had the good fortune to design our family ocean racer *Dorade*, launched in 1930, and other yachts described here. To me, at the time, *Dorade* did not seem radical. She differed from the International Rule race boats in her short ends. She retained their narrow beam and all outside lead ballast. If "conventional" meant "fisherman type", then so popular, she was radical in her construction. *Dorade*'s frames were steam bent rather than double-sawn fisherman style. They were closely spaced to give strength with light planking. She was a tough boat and our crew pushed her. The 1931 Fastnet was an example: we carried full sail when the rest of the fleet reefed, many deeply, and some were hove-to.

Fleets of yachts built in the 1930s, and others not quite as old, are now racing actively in many parts of the world. It has been like a new life to me. For a succession of years *Dorade,* and her near sisters have been restored in Porto San Stefano, Italy by a yard which is dedicated to restoration just like new. Four, pre 1939, have now been completed and a fifth, the 12 Metre, *Vim,* is now in the shop being readied for autumn 2004. The thrill of racing in *Dorade* has been almost like reliving our trial trips and our lucky breaks of 1931. To be back holding her tiller is excitement beyond description.

left One half of the legendary Sparkman & Stephens partnership, Olin Stephens attends the relaunching of Stormy Weather in Italy in 2001 – some 66 years after the yacht won the famous Fastnet Race.

To me, materials share with rules prime responsibility for the changes described here. Reverence for wood has a long history. Wood has qualities that cannot be duplicated. Only the extremely strong and rigid synthetics can much exceed wood's strength for weight. And wood naturally bends in curves admired by the eye and welcomed by the water. The human nose prefers the wood to possible alternatives. Surely sailors' love affair with wooden boats has fuelled their happy revival.

I share with the author his wonder and admiration for the fleet assembled at Cowes for the America's Cup Jubilee of 2001. A tribute to sailing history, it included the widest possible range of age, size, and type from *Partridge* to *Stealth* and with the latest of the Cup boats. During the week of sailing I found a chance to sail six of my "children", *Dorade, Stormy Weather, Zwerver, Valiant* and *Freedom*, one a day, racing. Never could I have hoped for this repetition. The thrill was that of the first trial trips.

Olin Stephens, March 2004

introduction

Twenty years ago, a classic yacht revival was little more than a hopeful aspiration, a much-talked about ambition which, like a mirage, vanished as soon as it seemed within reach. It was a precarious time for anyone working in the field, and it required a major leap of faith for any newcomers to get ensnared. Almost everyone involved with classic yachts - boatbuilders, owners, brokers, regatta organizers - was there out of love rather than out of any expectation of financial return. Many fell by the wayside, usually not from lack of skill but by economic necessity.

Yet a hard core of individuals had the determination and vision to weather the storm and hang on to their convictions against what were at times extremely poor odds. They did so not because they wanted to be part of a trend or movement, but simply because they believed in what they were doing. The fact that they eventually became the founding blocks of a major revival was icing on the cake. It's thanks to these visionary folk that the classic yacht movement has grown into one of the most remarkable phenomena in the world of sailing.

Now, classic yachts are as much a fashion accessory as a TVR sportscar or Armani coat. Celebrities as various as the Gucci sisters and Pete Townsend own them, while cutting edge designers such as Doug Peterson and Germán Frers spend their "quality time" racing them. And while it may be of little comfort to the owner of an old wooden boat struggling with a never ending renovation to know that Prada boss Patrizio Bertelli thinks it's worth spending $500,000 restoring a vintage yacht, there's little doubt that the rising prestige of these craft will ultimately benefit everyone. What was just an old boat 20 years ago is now potentially a valuable commodity, and that may be just the inspiration that's needed to get the sandpaper and varnish out yet again.

This book examines how classic yachts came out of the backwaters of neglect to become the stars of the sailing circuit.

right A long arduous restoration eventually paid off when the 1910 cutter *Hardy* joined the rest of the Old Gaffers on Britain's east coast. She was built by the once well-known UK yard of Summers & Payne.

Creation of a Legacy

August 1930 is the month any sailor worth their salt would love to relive. It was the month that saw the largest ever gathering of those spectacular and supremely graceful yachts known collectively as the "Big Class". And the place to be was the Solent, England's quintessential sailing playground, spiritual home of the sport of yachting itself. For it was on that narrow stretch of sheltered water between the Isle of Wight and England's southern coastline that many of the names that would go on to become part of sailing folklore had come to play – legendary yachts such as *Britannia, Westward, Shamrock, White Heather, Cambria, Astra,* and *Candida*. Even now, 70 years on, these vessels – some still surviving – still represent for many the pinnacle of sailing.

left The 1915 schooner *Mariette* is the largest yacht to have survived from the pen of America's greatest ever designer, Captain Nathaniel Herreshoff – also known as the "wizard of Bristol". Between 1893 and 1920, he was responsible for six successful America's Cup defenders.

Luckily, an English photographer by the name of Frank Beken, working out of Cowes on the Isle of Wight, was able to capture the unique sight of these yachts racing together. He had devised his own cleverly customized box camera – its shutter triggered by a rubber ball held in his mouth. In the United States, a similar role was fulfilled by Newport, Rhode Island photographer Stanley Rosenfeld, who documented the history of US yachting and the America's Cup in photos and words. The photographs of the US J-Class, *Enterprise, Rainbow, Weetamoe, Whirlwind, Yankee,* and *Ranger,* and the *British* Js *Endeavour, Shamrock V, Velsheda,* and *Endeavour II,* taken by Beken and Rosenfeld are among the most famous sailing images ever shot and symbolize the essence of what sailors and non-sailors have come to regard as "classic yachting".

But the sailing boom was not confined to the Solent. Throughout the 1930s, a succession of stunning yachts was launched off the drawing boards of Charles Nicholson in England, Nat Herreshoff in America, and Scotland's William Fife III, George Mylne and GL Watson – and a number from Scandinavia and Germany. It was also the decade of the legendary J-Class which had its brief but memorable flowering in just eight seasons from 1930 to 1937 by which time the interest in offshore sailing was flourishing with epoch-making racing and cruising yachts from the boards of the likes of young Olin Stephens, Jack Laurent Giles, and their European and Scandinavian counterparts such as Johan Anker, Henry Rasmussen and Willem de Vries.

The start of World War II ended these halcyon times and when yachting resumed in the mid-1940s, the world was a very different place. Technology had advanced, designs had evolved, and the social structure had been transformed. Before long, the advent of fibreglass would alter the face of yachting beyond recognition. With such momentous changes afoot, it's not difficult to see why the 1930s are regarded by many as "the golden age" of yachting. But how did the sport arrive at this apparent peak of evolution, and how real were its achievements?

The roots of sailing

Sailing for pleasure has its roots in water-laced Holland, where the first *jaght* races were recorded in the 17th century. Charles II and his court soon adopted the sport in the UK and, little more than 30 years after the War of Independence, in 1815, the first yacht was built in the United States. It was soon realized that racing results were as much about the type of boat being raced as the sailors who were racing them, and so a number of handicap rules were introduced in an attempt to level the playing field. It wasn't long, however, before designers learned how to exploit these rules and develop "unwholesome" designs such as, at one extreme, the typical American

"skimming dish" and, at the other extreme, the narrow-gutted, "plank-on-edge" European yachts. The former was capable of capsizing when carrying too much sail, while the latter had a tendency to behave more like a submarine than a boat.

It was not until the International Rule of 1907 that one formula stuck, and even then it was without the consent of the Americans. The International Rule was initiated by Britain's Yacht Racing Association – a precursor to the current Royal Yachting Association (RYA) – at a conference attended by representatives from 16 nations. The basis of the International Rule was a complicated formula which added up a yacht's vital statistics and produced a "measurement" that indicated which class the vessel belonged to, eg, 8-Metre or 12-Metre. Ten classes were specified, ranging from 5-Metres to 23-Metres, and boats could race within each class on equal footing – ie, without handicap. Confusingly, the figures themselves didn't relate directly to any real dimension on the actual boats but were merely abstract numbers produced by the formula – thus a typical 8-Metre is actually around 14m (46ft) long while a typical 12-Metre is nearer 20m (66ft) long: the boats may just as well be called 8-Sausages or 12-Dingbats.

The Metre yachts got off to a flying start after being selected as the principal classes in the 1908 Olympics, raced off Cowes. Within eight years of their launch, some 800 hulls had been built to the International Rule's specifications, and yards such as William Fife's in Scotland, Camper & Nicholson's in England, Anker & Jensen's in Norway, and a number of Scandinavian and German yards were building more Metre yachts than any other type. Over the years, designers inevitably found loopholes within the rule and the rule-makers twice altered it to prevent any "unwholesome" trends. But by 1933, the rule had reached its final formulation – one that is still in use to this day.

One important element of the International Rule was the inclusion of a Table of Scantlings, devised by Lloyd's Register, which ensured that all boats were built to adequate structural standards. It was a discipline that would serve European boatbuilders well and guarantee the survival of a remarkable number of craft.

In fact, the Europeans were one step behind the Americans, who had already devised their rule in 1903, thanks largely to the efforts of Nathanael Herreshoff, "the Wizard" of Bristol, Rhode Island. Although ignored on the other side of the Atlantic, the Universal Rule achieved similar goals to the International Rule, except that the resulting classes were denoted by a letter of the alphabet instead of a number – what was known, for example, as a 6-Metre in Europe was roughly equivalent to an R-Class in the USA, a 10-Metre to a P-Class, and so on. Absurdly, however, the rules were set up effectively in competition with each other, and it wasn't until the late 1920s that the International Rule was widely accepted in the USA – and even then only for the smaller classes.

left One of Britain's most revered designers was William Fife III, whose distinctive dragon motif was, from 1889, carved on every yacht to leave his yard on the Clyde. The 10-Metre *Tonino* was built for King Alfonzo of Spain in 1911 and transferred to Italy in 1914.

above The most successful designer to emerge from Scandinavia was Johan Anker, one half of the famous Anker & Jensen yard. Their first contribution to the new International Rule was the 9-Metre *Pandora*, launched in 1907.

previous page The 1896 cutter *Avel* was designed by that other giant of British pre-war yacht design, Charles Nicholson. For three decades the Camper & Nicholson yard was the largest yacht building company in the world.

next page Throughout the 1930s, the J-Class ruled the waves. They were the class chosen to race the America's Cup and soon became the queens of the race circuit. Charles Nicholson designed all three British J-Class challengers, including the 1934 *Endeavour*.

One of the weaknesses of the American system was that, unlike its European counterpart, there were no scantling requirements, which allowed the construction of highly-engineered but fundamentally weak craft. Not surprisingly, fewer Universal Rule boats have survived to become modern day classics.

Triumph of the J Boats

Where the Universal Rule triumphed, however, was in the choice of the J-Class – not the rule's largest, but arguably its most spectacular class – as the America's Cup boat for the 1930 races off Newport, Rhode Island. The choice was a transatlantic compromise. Several new 23-Metre yachts, such as the Fife-designed *Cambria*, and the Nicholsons *Astra*, and *Candida*, had recently been built to the International Rule in Britain, where the yachting fraternity was reluctant to dilute the fleet by introducing yet another type. But the lure of a transatlantic "big class" that could race in both the America's Cup and other regattas was strong and, as the Americans weren't about to adopt the Metre boats, Irish tea magnate Sir Thomas Lipton accepted a contest using boats built to the American formula, on condition that the Americans abided by European building strictures, ie, the Lloyd's scantlings. It was a done deal, and the first challenge took place off Newport in 1930 under the Universal Rule. The J-Class had arrived.

Although only 10 of them were ever built, six in the USA and four in Britain, and despite the fact that they raced for only eight seasons, the Js caught the public's imagination like no other class before or since. Although bigger yachts had been built before and have since, the Js' with their 40m (130ft) long hulls and towering bermudan rigs, which reduced their crew to the size of ants, and aggressively long ends, reaching out like an athlete stretching for the finish line, have been compared to the Marilyn Monroe, Rita Hayworth, and Greta Garbo of sailing. To many they were and are quite simply the ultimate yachts.

The 1930s were a time of great transition in terms of yacht design. In the US, that great giant of American sailing, Nat Herreshoff, designer of an unprecedented six successful America's Cup defenders, had retired. The famous schoonerman John Alden was at the height of his career. His yachts dominated ocean racing, meriting more entries in *Lloyd's Register of Yachts* than any other designer's. And the modern era of sailing was being ushered in by a precocious young designer by the name of Olin Stephens. The triumph of Stephens's slender yawl *Dorade* – designed when he was 21 years old – in the Bermuda and Fastnet Races of 1932 and 1933 was the start of a 50-year domination of the sport. His firm, Sparkman & Stephens, would design six defenders which between them would win eight America's Cup challenges, outstripping even Herreshoff's record.

In the UK, despite being in his 70s, the revered Scottish designer and builder William Fife III was still going strong at his yard at Fairlie,

and producing some of his finest work. Charles Nicholson was at the peak of his powers, designing all four of the British J-Class yachts as well as a long line of large cruising yachts. Indeed, from 1912 until 1939, the family business of Camper & Nicholsons in Gosport, opposite the naval base at Portsmouth, and Southampton, was the largest yacht building company in the world. Meanwhile, the shape of things to come was being sketched out by a young designer just setting up shop at Lymington on England's south coast. Through innovative pre-war designs such as *Maid of Malham*, Jack Laurent Giles was starting to open a new chapter in ocean racing.

A Swedish solution

A year after the International Rule was established in 1907, the Swedish Sailing Association (SSA) adopted its own rule, based on the so-called "skerry cruisers" class – those long, skinny yachts, with tall, narrow rigs designed to catch the winds blowing over Sweden's rock-strewn coasts. The SSA's Square-Metre rule restricted the yacht's sail area but not the length of the hull. Thus, in theory, as long as the sail area conformed to the yacht's class, its hull could be as long as the designer wanted. In practice, however, because the rules specified certain proportions of displacement to keel length, beam, and freeboard, a boat's length was to a certain extent self-regulating. Even so, a 22-Square-Metre yacht, for instance, might be anything from 8m to 11m (26ft to 36ft) long, depending on who designed her. The rule was revised in 1925 and some nine classes were eventually settled on, ranging from 15- to 150-Square-Metres.

The Scandinavians were also keen proponents of the Metre Boats, although whereas the rest of Europe favoured the 6-, 8-, and 12-Metres, they seemed to prefer the odd numbers. By 1930 Johan Anker had emerged as the pre-eminent Norwegian designer, excelling in both the Square-Metre and Metre classes and proving himself an able sailor, too, by winning a gold medal in the 12-Metre class at the 1912 Olympics. The popularity of Anker's 8.9m (29ft) Dragon design was spreading to the UK and would eventually be adopted as an Olympic class. Another popular Scandinavian design came from the pen of Sweden's Knud Reimers in 1932: the 8.3m (27ft 3in) *Tumlare*, which soon developed a following in Europe and as far afield as Australia. Meanwhile, that great Swedish innovator Fredrik Ljungström was just getting into his stride, and in 1934 revealed his latest invention: a double-layered sail that reefed on a revolving mast and spread open when sailing downwind to double the sail area. It became known as the Ljungström rig, and had a few ardent proponents.

The Dutch get together

In Holland, several companies had become established which would eventually join forces to form a unique boatbuilding conglomerate.

left The Swedish response to the so-called "Metre" rule was a Square-Metre Rule under which yachts were rated according to their sail area rather than their hull length. The 40 Square-Metre *Lola*, designed by Gustaf Estlander in 1924, was one of the smaller examples.

above One of the great Scandinavian innovators was Fredrik Ljungström who experimented with unstayed rigs, reverse sheers and rolled bulwarks. The 1939 *Facit* was one of the last boats designed by Johan Anker but shows a clear affinity to Ljungström.

previous page Better known for such impressive yachts as the ketch *Thendara*, Alfred Mylne also designed more modest craft. With her plumb bow and elegant counter, the 1903 cutter *Seagull* is a small gentleman's yacht typical of the era.

The DeVries and Van Lent yards in Holland provided the main boatbuilding expertise, while the office of Henri de Voogt specialized in design. Although still working in their own right in the 1930s, by 1949 the three firms joined with several others to created the Feadship group (First Export Association of Dutch Shipbuilders) to market their services overseas, much to the fury of the US boatbuilders whom they sought to undercut. The move was a resounding success, although it ultimately lead the companies away from wooden classics to aluminium and steel superyachts.

Long before then, the DeVries Lentsch yard had made a name for itself as builders of popular classes such as the Regenboog (or Rainbow) and the Pampus, as well as fine racing yachts such as the 6- and 8-Metre classes. And the family proved they weren't just boardroom sailors either when Willem deVries Lentsch Jnr won silver in the 8-Metre class in the 1928 Olympics in Amsterdam. Another notable DeVries success was the 15.24m (50ft) Sparkman & Stephens-designed yawl *Zeearend*, which won the Fastnet race in 1937.

On the other side of the world in New Zealand, the great rivalry between the two main boatbuilders, the Logans and the Baileys, continued unabated from the turn of the century until the Logan boatyard closed in 1910. By then an impressive fleet of what became known as the A-Class – boats more than 10.7m (35ft) long – had become established and continued to race on Auckland's Waitemata Harbour throughout the 1920s and '30s – albeit gradually updated from gaff to bermudan rig. The New Zealand yachting establishment was shocked out of its complacency, however, when a couple of "wharfies" decided to build a boat to take on the "yachties". Brothers Lou and Cyril Tercel were laughed at when they launched *Ranger* in 1938, but the 18m (60ft) cutter went on to thrash all the heavyweights of the A-Class and remained nigh unbeatable for nearly 30 years.

But the 1930s were not just about racing yachts. At the same time as the big class were competing on both sides of the Atlantic, a whole host of smaller, more accessible cruising yachts and day sailers was being commissioned from the famous racing designers. The most likely explanation for this explosion of enduring craft was that raw materials for wooden boatbuilding were still abundant and inexpensive and the labour required to build them was still relatively cheap. Production line methods were also becoming increasingly commonplace and could be applied, to a limited extent, to boat construction. It was a dream combination that produced a flurry of beautifully crafted vessels built out of the best materials available.

Cruising comes of age

As sailors began to stretch their horizons further afield, the Cruising Club of America was formed in the US in 1922 with the motto "nowhere is too far". Alden had by then proven his talents with his

above Ship's fittings, after centuries of development, were highly evolved by the 1930s and managed to combine aesthetic beauty with utility. Restorations, such as that of the Swedish yacht *Havsörnen*, must seek to replicate that combination.

right Swedish designer Tore Holm was responsible for a record number of Olympic winners between 1920 and 1948. *Havsörnen* was one of his successes and was recently auctioned at Sotheby's in London for over $200,000.

next page The 1963 *Fidelis* was one of the last great racing yachts built in wood. Designed by Vic Speight, she finally ended the legendary *Ranger*'s 30-year reign over New Zealand's yachting scene.

line of Malabar schooners (some 16 in all), initially built for himself and then sold on to new owners. In 1925, he joined the trend for smaller boats by going into production with the Malabar Junior, a 9.1m (30ft) bermudan sloop with the classic spoon bow and long counter that typified the designs of the era. With a small auxiliary engine and conservative rig, she was sold "ready to sail" – down to paraffin lamps and pilot books – for a modest $1,800 . It was another big step towards the popularization of sailing. The Juniors were built throughout the 1930s and, by the time the last one was launched in 1944, they numbered some 59 hulls.

Other affordable boats followed, such as the 10.7m (35ft) Weekender designed by Olin Stephens in 1937 and built at the Lawley yard in Massachusetts, and the 11m (36ft) Coastwise Cruiser produced the same year, and in direct competition, by the Alden yard.

But what must be the ultimate American production wooden cruising yacht emerged towards the end of the 1930s, although it only really got into full swing after World War II. The Concordia Yawl came into being after a hurricane swept across New England in 1938, wiping out hundreds of sailing boats in its path. One of the victims was a 11.9m (39ft) Norwegian Colin Archer design belonging to Llewellyn Howland, father of Waldo Howland, co-owner of the Concordia Boatyard in Massachusetts. Llewellyn asked his son to build him a replacement, to be designed by Waldo's partner Ray Hunt. The 11.9m (39ft) yawl that resulted was originally intended as a one-off, but the yacht's sweet shape and good sea-going abilities caught the attention of other sailors and before long the Concordia Yawl went into production. Very much part of the boats' attraction – aside from its pleasing overall design – was Waldo's legendary attention to detail, from the characteristic Pullman-style bunks in the saloon to the custom-made heater and the distinctive green corduroy upholstery.

By the time production of the Concordia ceased in the mid-1960s, more than 100 hulls had been built, most of them by the Abeking & Rasmussen yard in Germany. The yachts' reputation had been further enhanced by several high-profile race victories – including the 1954 Bermuda Race and a successful run at Cowes Week in the UK the following year – and it had become an undoubted cult classic.

Little boats, big reputations

On the other side of the Atlantic, the wooden boat bonanza produced its own collection of classics-in-the-making. One of the most prolific British designers of the 1930s was, ironically, an amateur. Thomas Harrison Butler was by profession an ophthalmic surgeon, but in his spare time liked to develop yacht designs. The result was a long line of pretty, seaworthy cruising yachts, starting with three "one-design" boats built in Hong Kong around 1910. Although he was made an Associate of the Institute of Naval Architects in 1938, T Harrison Butler

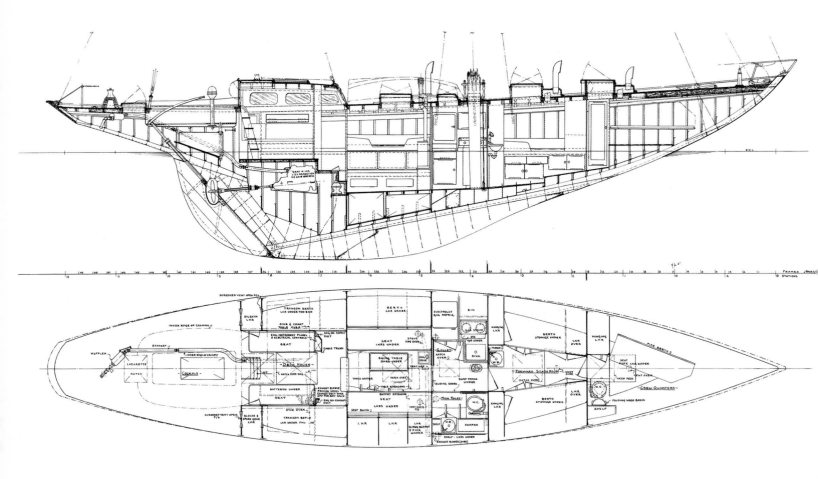

previous page *Zwerver*
went on to become one
of Holland's best-loved
yachts when she won the
prestigious Fastnet Race
in 1961, and many top
Dutch crew sailed
aboard her. By the
1970s, however, she
was outdated and
converted to charter
in the Mediterranean.

above *Zwerver* (originally
Zwerver II) was designed
by Sparkman & Stephens
and built at the De Vlijt
yard in Holland in 1956.
Her long, cutaway
forefoot was a sign of
things to come, although
her long overhangs
harked back to an
earlier era.

right The biggest name in
German yacht building is
Abeking & Rasmussen,
which has built 6,400
craft since it was founded
in 1907. The 1958 *Sintra*
was built by the yard
shortly before it switched
to building superyachts
and commercial vessels.

never asked for payment for his designs, apart from one guinea to
cover his expenses and a contribution to his favourite charity.

It was a sign of the times that one of his most successful designs
was also one of his smallest. The lines of the 6.4m (21ft) Zyklon, a
development of his 1919 Cyclone, were published in the British
magazine *Yachting Monthly* in 1937 and soon taken up by Alfred
Lockhart, wood joiners, near Brentford, Middlesex to the west of
London. The firm was ahead of its time in its use of production line
building practices and from the second boat onwards built the so-
called Z 4-Tonners in batches of 10. Harrison Butler's daughter, Joan
Jardine-Brown, visited the factory with her father in 1938–99 and
much later, in an article in UK-based Classic Boat magazine,
described how the hulls were assembled:

"They were built upside down on steel moulds incorporating the
ten stations. The oak frames were drawn from the steam box and set
in the jig to the correct curve and bevel for each station. Each
component was made from a jig or template including the full-length
planks, which were made in duplicate and then separated. Each item
was numbered, and each side of the boat was worked on
simultaneously, there being, in a large firm, no shortage of labour.

"The whole operation was streamlined. The oak stem, keel and
sternpost… and the deadwood, all made from templates, were fitted
to the steel mould and bolted to it temporarily. The pitch pine,

laminated stringers and shelves were steamed, shaped to the mould and held in place with cramps. The oak timbers were steamed, shaped in metal jigs and then slotted to the pre-notched keel and fastened to the stringers…"

Despite what must have seemed at the time like space age production techniques, the yachts were strongly built and many of the 52 Z4s produced by Lockharts survive to this day.

Another early pioneer of production building in the UK was the Berthon Boat Company in Lymington, on the Solent. In 1924 they started building what is thought to have been the first production yacht ever: the West Solent Restricted Class, whose numbers eventually reached more than 30. A decade later the yard came up with the design for an 11.3m (37ft) double-ended cruising yacht called the Gauntlet class. Like so many boats of that era, Gauntlets were impeccably built of pitch pine on oak with teak decks and mahogany-panelled interior, and, not surprisingly, soon acquired a devoted following. Berthon's produced 16 of the 12-Ton versions between 1934 and 1939, while another 22 were built in other denominations (ranging from 8- to 26-Ton) up until 1950.

Vertue rewarded

Jack Laurent Giles, the professional, was not above designing a "popular" boat either. He started with the 23ft (7m) Lymington One-Design (or L-Class) built from 1933 onwards. And then he drew the lines of a delightful 25-footer (7.6m) called *Andrillot*, built by Moody's on the Hamble River for Guernseyman Dick Kinnersly. *Andrillot* was much smaller than most of her creator's subsequent commissions – including the 33m (110ft) *Blue Leopard* – yet this unpretentious gaff cutter is still described by some as his masterpiece. Another 10 hulls were built to the design prior to 1939, but it wasn't until after the war that it finally became known as the Vertue class – so named due to the fifth, *Epeneta*, having won the 1940 Vertue Cup, an annual log-writing prize presented since 1927 by the Little Ship Club of London in honour of its librarian of that name.

But, like Ray Hunt's Concordia Yawl, Laurent Giles's design had to wait for post-war prosperity to kick in before cementing its place in history. From 1945 to 1950 27 Vertues were built and, at the peak of production, 11 in 1963. A number of epic voyages have been made on these little world-girdlers, the most famous being Humphrey Barton's transatlantic crossing on *Vertue XXXV* in 1950. Barton's adventures became the subject of a book named after the boat, which confirmed the design's status as the quintessential small cruising yacht in the UK.

After World War II it soon became clear that wooden boats everywhere were living on borrowed time. Demographic changes meant that labour costs were rising in the West, while the supply of good timber needed to build these beautiful yachts began to dry up.

left More than 100 Concordia yawls were built in the 1940s and 50s, most of them by Abeking & Rasmussen. The 1938 American design was one of the earliest yachts to be production-built but was eventually eclipsed by cheaper glassfibre hulls.

above The Vertue class, designed by Jack Laurent Giles, has become a cult classic in Britain. At just 25ft (7.6m) long, the boats have travelled the world and were eventually adapted for construction in fibreglass. Built in 1937, *Sally II* is one of the oldest of the type.

next page American designer Philip Rhodes was still designing wooden boats well into the 1950s, including the 56ft (17m) sloop *Caper*. A year after *Caper* was launched, in 1957 the Rhodes-designed *Bounty II* launched the fibreglass revolution in the United States.

On the other hand, society as a whole was more affluent than it had ever been and the potential market for small- to medium-sized boats was growing apace. As the austere 1950s became the affluent '60s, what was needed was a cheap method of producing hulls in large numbers. While the production methods developed before the war had made significant strides in that direction, post-war labour and timber costs largely negated those gains.

A hot idea

One of the first attempts at mass production was the use of hot moulding. Simply put, hot moulding consisted of applying several layers (usually three) of wood veneer over a male mould, bonding them together with Resorcinol glue and heating the whole lot in an autoclave to "cure" the adhesive. The resulting structure was remarkably strong and needed little in the way of internal strengthening. The method had long been used in aircraft construction where its high strength-to-weight ratio was a boon, but was not commercially applied to boats until after the war.

One of the first builders to see its potential was Fairey Marine on the Hamble River in the UK who, as Fairey Aviation, were already applying the technique to aircraft building. They started churning out hot-moulded Firefly dinghies by the hundreds from 1946 onwards, and by 1956 the yard had applied the same principle to another, larger cruising yacht by Uffa Fox. The 7.9m (26ft) *Atalanta* was an innovative design, with its rolled deck and centre cockpit, and some 81 hulls were built by Fairey's in the first three years of production. By the time construction ceased in 1968, nearly 200 had been produced.

Hot moulding alone was never going to be enough, however, to fulfill the growing demand worldwide for cheap boats of all sizes. That would be left to the latest miracle material: fibreglass. Predictably, there is much heated debate about who built the first fibreglass boat, but the general consensus is that it was Ray Greene of Toledo, Ohio, who produced a polyester resin and fibreglass dinghy in 1942. The US Navy was quick off the mark and ordered a pair of 8.5m (28ft) personnel carriers which were launched six years later. The actual moulding and curing of these hulls took a mere six hours, a contemporary report noted, compared to the 360 hours a similar wooden hull would have taken six men to build.

"Frozen snot"

But it was Taylor Winner of Trenton, New Jersey, who in 1945 produced the first "series" of production fibreglass boats with his line of PlastiCraft dinghies and runabouts. By 1947 the world's first "plastic" sailboats, the 4.9m (16ft) *Rebel* and the 3.8m (12ft 6in) *Swan*, both built by Ray Greene, were in production. It was the start of the most far-ranging revolution the boatbuilding industry had ever seen.

previous page One of the most prolific British designers of the 1930s was an ophthalmic surgeon by the name of Thomas Harrison Butler. There is some debate whether *Judy Anne* is a true Harrison Butler, but if not she certainly imitates his style pretty well...

above Another popular pocket cruiser was the 25ft (7.6m) Folkboat, conceived by the Royal Gothenburg Yacht Club. Designed in 1939, it was built of wood until the mid-1970s when it made a successful transition to fibreglass. Some 2,500 Folkboats have been built worldwide.

right One of the new boys on the block in the 1930s was British designer Robert Clarke who would later draw OSTAR winner *Sir Thomas Lipton* as well as Francis Chichester's *Gipsy Moth V. Mystery of Meon* was the first of his designs to be built.

It would be another four years before fibreglass boats were available in the UK, and that was when W&J Tod of Weymouth in Dorset produced a line of experimental 3.7m (12ft) dinghies in 1951. Uffa Fox, ever at the cutting edge of design and technology, followed suit in 1952 with a one-off Flying Twenty, which was soon followed by a batch of fibreglass Flying Fifteens, all built by Halmatic near Portsmouth, Hampshire. Half a century later, the evergreen Flying Fifteens now number around 3700. Fox's choice of builders was astute. Halmatic would go on to be one of the leading players in the development of the medium, consistently breaking records for the size of boats they were building in fibreglass.

From sailing dinghies it was a small but significant step to producing auxiliary cruising boats, and the Coleman Boat & Plastics Co in California were the first to do so with the 12.4m (40ft 10in) *Bounty II*. The yacht was intended to follow on the success of the original *Bounty*, designed before the war by Philip Rhodes for production in wood, and indeed its appearance at the New York Boat Show in 1957 marked a new era in yachting history. Henceforth, fibreglass – or "frozen snot", as Nat Herreshoff's son L Francis famously described it – would become increasingly the norm for boats of all sizes. Some made the transfer from wood very naturally, such as the Sou'Wester series built by the Hinckley Boat Company in New England, which evolved from a highly successful production wooden boat into an even more successful production fibreglass boat. Increasingly, though, as the potential of the new material was realized and design ideas moved on, the new boats broke away from their traditional roots and acquired a style all of their own.

In Europe, Dutch designer EG Van de Stadt was one of the earliest to exploit the benefits of the new technology. His Pionier and Excalibur classes never made any pretence of being anything other than fibreglass, nor did the French Bénéteau range, which from 1964 grew to dominate the market. In the UK, by contrast, the heavily-built Nicholson 36 – Camper & Nicholsons' early foray into mass production of 1962 – seemed to be all too obviously a wooden boat at heart, even down to having timber decks and superstructure. Significantly, perhaps, both the Nic 36 and her more commercial, all-fibreglass little sister, the Nic 32, have since become classics in their own right.

Wood eclipsed by glass

The new technology's advance was extraordinarily fast. Whereas in 1950 there where just 22 fibreglass boats at the New York Boat Show, just 11 years later they would account for more than half the craft exhibited. Similarly in Britain, the percentage of fibreglass boats at the London Boat Show leapt from 17 in 1956 to around 70 per cent in 1979. No wonder so many traditionalists were alarmed: the sheer pace of the relatively unproven method's sweeping dominance must have

seemed like an affront to the centuries of evolution and proven worth of wooden boats. From being *the* primary means of building yachts, in the space of half a generation, wood had become marginalized.

As construction techniques evolved, so inevitably did the boats' design. Since the 1890s, designers such as Nat Herreshoff and Charles Sibbick in England had played with the idea of fin keels and even experimented with bulb keels – the recently-restored Sibbick 5-Tonner *Bona Fide* is a rare example of one such craft. When launched, in 1895, she was at least 50 years before her time. But these were one-off freaks. Essentially, the shape of boats had altered little since the end of the "plank-on-edge" designs of the 1890s.

Yacht design evolved apace in the 1930s on both sides of the Atlantic, epitomized in 1937 when Laurent Giles designed *Maid of Malham* for British sailor John Illingworth – often referred to as the founding father of modern ocean racing. *Maid* put many traditionalists' noses out of joint because of her cutaway keel, and controversial masthead rig (virtually all yachts at that time had the forestay fixed some distance below the top of the mast) – both of which were deemed deeply unseamanlike. They would soon become the norm.

Worse was to come after the war, however, when Illingworth ordered a new yacht from Laurent Giles. *Myth of Malham* did away with any pretence at conventional beauty but undoubtedly made the most of the UK's Royal Ocean Racing Club (RORC) rating rule to which she was built. With her chopped-off stern, her stubby bow, lack of sheer, almost vertical topsides, and small mainsail area, she broke the mould of sailboat design – and many a traditionalists' heart in the process. She also won the Fastnet Race twice in a row, in 1947 and 1949. As Illingworth later said, "*Maid* was good, but *Myth* set the fashion."

The new trend was set and by 1965, when American designer Dick Carter's lightweight, almost dinghy-like RORC Rule boat *Rabbit*, won the Fastnet, the tide had turned irrevocably. Two years later, Olin Stephens attacked even the old International Rule, by separating the rudder from the keel on his America's Cup 12-Metre defender *Intrepid*.

The Wizard departs

For many of the yards that had built some of the most famous boats of the pre-war era, the end had already come. That great symbol of American yachting pride, the Herreshoff Boat Manufacturing Company, had been sold off by the Herreshoff family in 1924. The firm managed to survive the war on military contracts but finally shut down its slipways in 1945. Nat Herreshoff himself died in 1938. Likewise, the legendary Lawley yard, founded in 1866 and builders of many a fine racing yacht, finally gave up construction in 1945. Meanwhile, the Nevins boatyard on City Island, New York, responsible for such Olin Stephens classics as *Stormy Weather* and *Brilliant*, changed hands during the war and lost its founder Henry Nevins.

left With the advent of plywood in the 1950s and 1960s, yacht designs changed to suit the new material. The great British designer/author Maurice Griffiths came up with the *Golden Hind* in 1965, originally built in plywood and later adapted to fibreglass.

above What the *Golden Hind* lacked in elegance it more than made up for in comfort. The chunky 31-footer had more space below decks than many much larger predecessors. It was seaworthy too, and soon acquired a reputation as a dependable little globetrotter.

next page By the end of the 1970s it was all over for many wooden boats. The cheapness of fibreglass combined with the ease of maintenance brought yachting to a larger public than ever before and spelled the end for traditional yachts. Or did it?

The pattern was the same in Europe. The German invasion of Norway in the spring of 1940 put yachting on hold for several years, and within a few months the country also had to say farewell to its pre-eminent yacht designer, Johan Anker, who died at the Red Cross Hospital in Oslo in October 1940. Meanwhile, in the UK even the finest yacht building yard in the land could not survive the death of its most revered designer. William Fife died in 1944 and, when the yard at Fairlie reopened after the war it was under a different name and new management. And in 1945 the much-loved Harrison Butler died.

Condemned to muddy creeks

But while the yards and designers that created this vibrant era of yachting were gradually eclipsed, the boats they had produced struggled – often seemingly against all odds – to stay alive. Many were modernized through the addition of boxy doghouses, usually simply fixed as rather ghastly extensions to the existing cabin top. Some, such as the irreplaceable *Shamrock V*, the first British J-Class yacht ever built, suffered the indignity of having their bulwarks and cabins raised wholesale to create more space below decks and give them a more "contemporary" look. But probably first thing on the list of any modernization programme, for boats that had it, was that cumbersome gaff rig. The greater efficiency of bermudan sails to windward had won most sailors over, and wooden masts and cotton sails were discarded and replaced by aluminium and Dacron faster than you could say "bandwagon".

As the older wooden boats became more and more outmoded, so their sale value fell and so did the incentive to maintain them. It was a vicious circle: the more unloved they were, the less they were well kept, and the less they were well kept, the more unwanted they became. Eventually, in England and elsewhere, many were dragged up muddy creeks and turned into houseboats – including *Lulworth*, and the British J-Class yachts *Velsheda* and *Endeavour*, once known by her owner Tom Sopwith as his "the darling jade". But whatever indignities were visited upon these once-proud craft, it was usually better that they were used for *something* because that at least kept them from being broken up. None of the six American Js survived the war. Even the most famous yacht of them all, the original schooner *America*, winner of the 1851 race that spawned the America's Cup, succumbed to the elements when her shed collapsed in a heavy snow fall.

By the end of the 1960s, wood had been almost completely eclipsed by fibreglass and traditional design concepts had been outmanoeuvred and outsailed by the "moderns". Dick Carter had triumphed over Nat Herreshoff, and nature's most versatile material, wood, had given way to resin-soaked fibreglass cloth. The very concept of a "classic yacht" seemed little more than an optimistic play on words. Wooden yachts from being loved became liabilities.

the Revival is Born

In the summer of 1967 Dick Wagner, an architect at the Boeing aircraft factory in Seattle, left his secure office job and set up a business nearby, renting out the wooden boats he had collected from local boatyards and then restored. As the yards gradually closed down, he realized that a way of life was disappearing and that his little fleet had acquired a rather special significance. His business was called The Old Boathouse and was founded with a simple purpose. "My wife Colleen said to me that if we don't do anything, by the time our children are grown, there won't be any wooden boats left," he told a local TV station. "We just wanted to hold on to the heritage for a little while longer."

left The classic yacht revival was as much about a return to standards as anything to do with a type of boat. The intricacies of a ship's wheel at the Clayton Antique Boat Show in New York shows the attention to detail that many feared had become a thing of the past.

Three years earlier, on the other side of the US in Clayton, New York, Allan Youngs and his wife were walking near their home by the St Lawrence River when they spotted an old wooden launch sitting on blocks in a corner of the nearby Thousand Islands Marina. Smitten by her traditional construction and classic lines, they bought the boat, and persuaded the yard to restore it for them. When they picked the boat up the following spring, they were so delighted with their new acquisition that they decided to organize an event where they and other like-minded folk could display their boats.

The first Antique Boat Show in 1965 was attended by 20 craft, several of whose owners turned up in period costume. The event had enough support to prompt the Clayton Chamber of Commerce and the Clayton Village Board to offer dock space and free publicity, and the following year nearly 40 boats attended. The year after that it was 100, and the show had filled up the whole of the town quay and most of the dock at Thousand Islands Marina.

Old World stirrings

Back in the Old World similar stirrings were taking place, as the ghost of sailboats past showed signs of waking from its 30-year sleep. Although the new marinas being built around the shores of Britain were gradually filling up with identical white fibreglass boats flying identical white sails, a few contrary folk were rediscovering the joys of sailing heavy old wooden boats with archaic tanned, cotton sails. In 1958, long after most of the world had been wooed by the benefits of the bermudan rig, a group of British die-hards had banded together to organize a couple of races for gaff-rigged boats.

According to maritime historian Robert Simper, "this was the spark that started the forest fire of enthusiasm for the gaff rig". The Old Gaffers' Association (OGA) was formed later that year, the very name of the new organization reflecting its anachronistic aspirations. Within a few months, across the Channel in France, the first fibreglass yacht from the Bénéteau factory would be launched, signalling the start of a flood of characterless glassfibre boats which would soon swamp harbours all over the world. Yet, just as the fibreglass revolution was beginning to elbow out wood and bermudan was prevailing over gaff, there were those who were staging a spirited defence of both material and rig.

The seeds sown by these individuals following their own conviction, often in isolation, took time to become a movement, let alone a revival. It was even longer before anyone knew whether the movement was more than a reactionary flash in the pan. Even now it's difficult to pinpoint the exact significant events that led to the boats of yesteryear being brought in from the cold. The great classic yacht revival as we now know it was really just a collection of individuals realizing their dreams.

left The revival in Britain was initially focused on its wealth of vernacular craft, such as the famous Falmouth Working Boats, the last in Europe to still work under sail. Many, such as *Boy Willie*, had been tuned up for racing in lively local races.

above Within three years the Clayton Antique Boat Show in New York had grown from an informal gathering of friends into one of the highlights of the boating calendar. Its success was one of the first signs of the emerging classic-boat revival.

The power of dreams

Dreams do, however, have power. Wagner's Old Boathouse went on to become the foundation stone of the Wooden Boat Centre in Seattle, one of the main focuses of wooden boatbuilding on the West Coast of the United States. The centre now owns 150 small craft, most of which are rented to the public, offering a hands-on experience of sailing classic boats. It also runs dozens of practical courses in everything from lofting to tool-making, as well as organizing annual regattas and hosting a lively circuit of public speakers.

Meanwhile, the Clayton Antique Boat Show began by Youngs continued to grow, regularly hosting 125 boats as well as a large number of exhibitors. The Antique Boat Museum was founded in 1971 (originally as the Thousand Islands Shipyard Museum) as an offshoot of the show and now exhibits around 200 classic boats. It, too, has a busy programme of boatbuilding and sailing courses on its two-acre riverside "campus". In 2004 the Clayton Antique Boat Show celebrated its 40th anniversary, making it the oldest classic boating event in continuous operation in the world.

As for the Old Gaffers, the association now boasts branches in France, Germany, Holland, and Australia. Its core membership of 1400 is in the UK where its main events on The Solent and the East Coast are attended by more than 100 boats. Over the years, there have been divisions and infighting over contentious issues, such as allowing fibreglass boats into the association (leading to the popular expression, "there's nothing naffer than a plastic gaffer") and, more recently, giving bermudan boats associate membership. But through it all the organization has continued to grow. "The OGA was like a snowball rolling downhill," said Simper, former president of the OGA. "Bits kept dropping off, but the main theme kept getting larger."

It might seem strange to trace back the roots of the swanky classic yachts which now parade the French Riviera to a dinghy shop in Seattle or a riverboat regatta in New York state or a working boat race in Essex. Yet that is almost certainly where the shift of consciousness which led to a new appreciation of the traditional values embodied by the classic yacht movement originated. It started as a straightforward reaction to the consumerism of the 1950s and '60s and the advent of mass production which led to a flood of cheaply-produced goods – including boats. By contrast, the quality of materials and craftsmanship in wooden boats symbolized many of the values that had been lost in the rush for material possessions.

Plank on Frame

Paul Lipke in his book *Plank on Frame* (a snapshot of wooden boatbuilding in the United States during the late 1970s, published in 1981) suggests how seriously these early revivalists took their task, and how aware they were of its significance within the wider context. "There are implications about our whole society if these boats are allowed to fall into obscurity," he wrote. "The grace of any good vessel underway, the integrity of her design and construction within her intended purpose symbolize for devotees a culture-wide return to crafts and values. The aesthetic qualities of wood, both as a boatbuilding material and in light of environmental and energy concerns, only serve to underline this appeal. To care about these boats is to say you care in general; apathy is unacceptable."

Broadly speaking, the movement in the United States was split into two factions: the older, time-served boatbuilders who were continuing a tradition handed down from one generation to the next, and the younger, idealistic newcomers. Among the younger group, the revival was associated with the back-to-the-earth movement, and its proponents were often bohemian drop-outs without necessarily the skills or the funds to tackle large projects. A tradition of building small but exquisitely-crafted dinghies and canoes thus developed, in areas such as Puget Sound on the US West Coast and Maine on the East.

above The schooner *Brilliant* remained in superb condition throughout thanks to the stewardship of the Mystic Seaport Museum in Connecticut, USA. The museum has been an inspiration for traditional boat aficionados since it was founded in 1929.

above right The interior of *Brilliant* is still almost unchanged from when she was launched in 1931. Designed by Olin Stephens when he was just 22 years old, the yacht was built strong enough to withstand being rolled over in a hurricane.

below right The close spacing of *Brilliant*'s frames speaks of a yacht designed for ocean sailing. Her design is said to have been inspired by the ideas of British author Claud Worth – except that most of her ballast is in the keel rather than the bilge.

next page The enthusiasm generated by the first Port Townsend Wooden Boat Festival in 1977 took everyone by surprise. The event has become one of the centrepieces of the American revival.

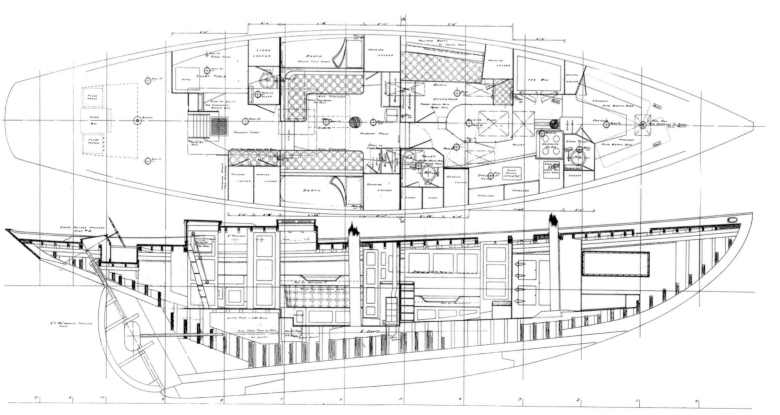

Soon, small boatbuilding shops were opening all around the US, often occupied by no more than one man and his dog and sometimes with little basis in financial reality. It would take time for the serious players to emerge from the dreamers. Companies such as the Brooklin Boatyard and Rockport Marine, both in Maine, were established as early as 1960 and 1962 and are still going strong 40 years later. Many more, however, were not so fortunate.

Alongside these new shops, training centres were set up to teach the new devotees the skills of what had until recently been deemed a dying art. The most influential was the Apprenticeshop at the Maine Maritime Museum in Bath (now based in Rockland). The old apprenticeship system had long since fallen by the wayside in the US as elsewhere, but there were still old-timers willing to pass on their knowledge. Most notable among these was the legendary John Gardner, who from 1969 until his retirement 26 years later at 90 built up the small craft programme at Mystic Seaport, in Connecticut, and wrote copious articles and books on the subject.

By 1981, Lipke estimated that there were some 1500 professional wooden boatbuilders in the US, and, including amateur projects, he guessed that there were at least 15,000 traditional wooden boats under construction in the country. Not bad for a breed that was thought to be verging on extinction only 15 years before.

Meanwhile, the Clayton Antique Boat Show was followed by myriad similar events at, among others, Mystic in Connecticut, Cape Cod in Massachusetts, and the "three saints" (Santa Cruz, San Diego and San Francisco) in California. A taste of what was to come was the first Opera House Cup Regatta on Nantucket Island in 1973. Organized by the restaurant of the same name, it was intended as a knockabout race for a few of the local classics. It subsequently developed into one of the major events in the yachting calendar with as many as 80 yachts taking part. Past winners include legendary yachts such as the Sparkman & Stephens schooner *Brilliant* and 12-Metres *Gleam*, and *American Eagle*.

Enter *Woodenboat*

One of the notable early successes on the West Coast was the first Wooden Boat Festival held at Port Townsend, near Seattle, in 1977. Nearly 5000 people and more than 100 boats attended the three days of lectures, demonstrations, and races, with events ranging from bronze casting to folk dancing. The response took everyone by surprise – including the organizers – and was the clearest indication to date that the much-talked-about revival really was under way.

Another major landmark in this resurgence was the publication of the first magazine devoted entirely to old wooden boats. Launched in 1974 by former boatbuilder Jon Wilson *The Wooden Boat* enjoyed phenomenal success almost from its first issue. Within a year it had

attracted 8000 subscribers, and by the end of its third year its circulation had risen to an impressive 25,000. By 1981 *WoodenBoat*, as it was by then known, had moved to grandiose new offices on a 60-acre estate overlooking Eggemoggin Reach in Maine. There, with the participation of eminent local figures such as yacht designer Joel White and author Maynard Bray, the magazine not only continued to expand but also set up its own programme of boatbuilding and sailing courses. Within a few years, its circulation was more than 100,000, where it has remained ever since. Clearly, as Wilson wrote in his very first editorial, it was a magazine "whose time has come".

Classic boat enthusiasts in Europe could only look on in amazement and envy. Despite the early gestures from a few committed individuals, the revival in Europe was much slower to get under way, and, when it eventually did, it took a rather different form to its New World counterpart. Whereas in America efforts were concentrated on smaller craft and gradually spread to bigger yachts, the rebirth in France and Britain started among the country's indigenous working boats which, in Britain at least, had survived in surprising number – albeit converted for cruising or as houseboats. Almost all of these craft had originally been gaff-rigged, and thus the movement was often identified with "old gaffers", although in due course it would spread well beyond that bracket.

In France, the revival initially focused on the country's *patrimoinage*, or cultural heritage which meant, inevitably, its long lineage of working boats – most of which had been destroyed either during the war or soon after. The influential magazine *Chasse-Marée*, founded in 1981 by editor Bernard Cadoret and a group of friends, lavishly produced and with no advertising, soon became the definitive historic journal about traditional boats and found favour among French and non-French readers alike. Starting with a circulation of 7000 in 1981, it rose to 20,000 in just four years, and to 40,000 by 1996, of which a remarkable 40 per cent were subscribers.

Meanwhile, the first traditional boat festival at Pors-Beach in Brittany in 1980 gave the first glimpse of the tidal wave of French public support for the movement. After three editions the event outgrew the town, and in 1986 *Chasse-Marée* organized the first festival of sail at Douarnenez. The rows of tan sails and black-painted hulls lining the scenic Breton harbour were a heart-stopping sight and Douarnenez immediately became one of the biggest events in the classic boat calendar. By 1988, some 200,000 visitors and thousands of boats were invading the town.

The same year that *Chasse-Marée* was launched in Brittany, another group of sailors in the South of France at the glitzy resort of St-Tropez was concocting a different plan. One night in 1981, over a few drinks, Jean Lorain and Dick Jayson challenged each other to a race from St-Tropez to a buoy located five miles off Pampelonne and

back. The buoy was called La Nioulargue. In the race the next day between Lorain's 12-Metre *Ikra* and Jayson's *Swan 44*, the 12-Metre won. The next year some 23 boats took part in what was already being referred to as the Nioulargue regatta. By 1984 more than 100 yachts, including the British J-Class *Velsheda*, had joined the fun.

La Nioulargue in St-Tropez

The event quickly became established as the fashionable regatta to attend. For, as much as it was about racing, La Nioulargue was about being moored up at the heart of one of the most glamorous resorts in the world. The classic part of the fleet was always given pride of place, and the rows of yachts, with their glinting hardware and glowing woodwork made an impressive sight by any standard. These boats were there not just as racing machines, but as objects of beauty to be displayed and admired. There's no doubt that the Nioulargue spectacle persuaded more than a few potential owners to "go classic" – and most would have been persuaded on the quayside rather than on the water.

In Britain the enthusiasm for old working boats had developed sufficiently by 1977 for author and sailor John Mellor to write: "In Britain today there is an upsurge of interest in old working sailing boats, to the extent that their prices are rocketing in the style of vintage cars." He went on to note that "the most interesting thing of all, however, is that the boats are exactly the same. No plastic hulls; no lofty bermudan sailplans; no titanium rod rigging; just the same old wooden, gaff-rigged boats as always." Significantly, however, Mellor had to go to *Woodenboat*, to have these words published as there was nothing comparable in the UK. It would be another 10 years before Britain launched its own specialist magazine.

Likewise, Dutch interest initially focused on the country's rich diversity of working boats. From its famous flat-bottomed working *lemsteraken* on the IJsselmeer to its powerful *klippers*, offshore trading ships, an astonishing number of craft had survived and were being restored with typically Dutch zeal. Craft that were once used to carry sand and dung were transformed into pristine yachts and, because so many were built of steel in the first place, they could be raced very hard indeed. It wasn't until 1982 that an association, the Vereniging Klassieke Scherpe Jachten, was formed specifically for classic, long-keeled yachts.

Crabbers and Shrimpers

The interest in traditional boating manifested itself in other, more curious, ways. British amateur designer Roger Dongray started a mini sailing revolution in the early 1970s when he designed a 7.3m (24ft) gaff cutter for his personal use. Although the prototype was built of plywood, the design caught the attention of a pair of British entrepreneurs, Peter Keeling and Ken Robertson, who wanted to build it in fibreglass: the first Cornish Crabber was launched in 1974 and was

pages 52–3 The seeds of the Mediterranean classic yacht circuit were sown during a race off St Tropez in 1981 which led to the Nioulargue regatta. The Camper & Nicholson ketch *Orion*, restored at La Spezia in 1979, was one of the pioneers of the new movement.

previous page One of the boats to buck the trend for all things plastic was *Chloe May*, launched in Fowey, UK, in 1982. Built by Peter Nash to a design by West Country designer Percy Dalton, she was built in solid timber and was traditional right through to her big gaff heart.

above Drastic action was needed in France to replenish their stock of indigenous craft – most of which had been destroyed during and after World War II. *Chasse Marée* magazine masterminded a drive to rebuild craft such as the bisquine *La Granvillaise*.

right The resurgence of working boats soon filtered across to sailing yachts, particularly in Britain, where the original *Cornish Crabber*, launched in 1974, gradually expanded into a popular range of boats. *Aliesje* is a 7-ton Pilot Cutter, the largest of the line.

an immediate hit. It was followed six years later by the even more popular Cornish Shrimper. Suddenly the concept of a plastic gaffer had entered the mainstream and eventually whole rows of the boats were to be seen bobbing at their moorings in harbours and creeks around the country. Although this was probably not what John Scarlett and the other luminaries had in mind when they founded the OGA, there's no doubt that these "plastic gaffers" played a significant role in bringing an awareness of gaff rig and traditional boats to a wider audience.

With Britain's manufacturing base in decline and unemployment rocketing, it must have taken a substantial leap of faith to start a school dedicated solely to wooden boatbuilding. Yet that is exactly what happened when the International Boatbuilding Training College in Lowestoft, Suffolk, opened in 1975. Despite being born in such apocalyptic times, however, the school not only survived but has gone on to become one of the most respected training centres in the world. Recently a rival opened its doors in Dorset's Lyme Regis, the Boat Building Academy where tutors such as Jack Chippendale, foremost builder of racing dinghies, passes on long-learnt skills.

In the mid-'80s, however, the UK was still awaiting the revival on a US scale. The wooden boat movement was struggling to take off, something designer Iain Oughtred was keenly aware of. In 1986 he collated a builders' guide based on the same premise as Lipke's *Plank on Frame* published in the US five years earlier. In *Wooden Boatbuilding in Britain*, Oughtred bemoaned the lack of a "rallying point" for the movement. "On the East Coast of the USA the magazine *WoodenBoat* has achieved an almost mystical position with a devoted readership…" he wrote. "There is no British equivalent and so naturally many of the British boatbuilders read *WoodenBoat* and as a result are influenced by its philosophy and designs." Within a year, his prayers were answered. Former schoolteacher Pete Greenfield started up *Classic Boat* magazine from his home near Falmouth in Cornwall, and soon had a small but devoted following. The same year a classic boat regatta was started at Shotley Point Marina in Suffolk, followed in 1988 by a similar event in Falmouth, Cornwall. At last, it seemed, the long-awaited British resurgence was starting to take place.

Norwegian wood

By the mid-80s events were springing up all over Europe; the first Wooden Boat Festival in 1984 at Risør in the south of Norway grew into one of the key classic boat attractions. In the Mediterranean a whole series of regattas started to take shape, with La Nioulargue at its core: the Raduno Vele d'Epoca at Imperia, on the Italian riviera and the Cannes Régates Royales on the French. In Italy, the newly-formed Italian Vintage Sailboat Association, Associazione Italiana Vele d'Epoca, set new rules to help regulate the racing – rules that form the basis of classic yacht racing all over the Mediterranean.

previous page The classics got a new, blue-water playground with the start of the Antigua Classics in the late 1980s. The John Alden yawl *Lucia A* enjoys the steady Caribbean breeze with race organizer Kenny Coombs installed as skipper.

above The renewed interest in boats of yesteryear led to a demand for skills to match. While many doomsayers insisted the art of wooden boatbuilding had been lost forever, colleges were soon producing a new generation of skilled trainees.

Right Who says wooden boatbuilding is dead? The International Boatbuilding College in Lowestoft, UK, was founded in the mid-1970s and run as a semi-commercial boat yard, with at least half a dozen wooden boats in build at any one time.

It took a little longer for what the OGA's Robert Simper had called the "forest fire of enthusiasm" to spread to Australia. The first wooden boat festival was held at Goolwa near Adelaide in 1989 and, from small beginnings, grew to eventually number 250 boats and 10,000 visitors. Larger gatherings in Sydney and Hobart followed.

But by far the biggest event in the traditional boat calendar was created by the French team behind *Chasse-Marée* magazine and the popular Douarnenez festival. After running for just two years, it soon became clear that the Douarnenez event was outgrowing the town and that once again a new venue would have to be found. The result was the Brest '92 festival, the largest gathering of traditional boats the world had ever seen: 2200 boats from all over Europe ranging from French bisquines to British bawleys, and one-and-a-half million visitors over five days of non-stop festivities. It was only beaten by the next festival at Brest in 1996 when 2500 boats and four million people attended. It was said that there were so many boats that year on the feeder race from Brest to the smaller regatta at Douarnenez that you could have walked there by just hopping from one boat to the next.

A boat on every coast

As if gathering Europe's existing traditional craft together was not enough, by 1992 *Chasse-Marée* had launched an innovative new scheme to replenish France's stock of traditional craft. Every town that had ever had an indigenous type of working boat was asked to restore or build a replica of one. The *Bateaux des Côtes* (lit: boats from around the coasts) scheme stimulated a great deal of civic pride and, thanks largely to local council funding, some 80 restorations and new-builds were launched in time to attend Brest '92.

With the Millennium fast approaching, traditional craft were clearly in no danger of being forgotten in the fanfare for the new century. The old skills were there. Since the advent of fibreglass, there had been ongoing talk of how traditional boatbuilding skills were dying out, as if it were a mystical trade whose secrets lay forever buried in the 1930s. The reality was that there was a more or less continuous stream of one-off wooden boats being built all over the world. Admittedly, many of these were amateur-built, but they at least proved that those skills were still there to be learned and practised. In France the shipwrights' mallets rang with the sound of oakum being forced into the seams of a local craft from Normandy to the Med, and also in the UK where old-style boats were being built such as the Murray Peterson schooner *Mary Bryant* and the Percy Dalton cutter *Chloe May*, both launched in 1981.

Engineless dreamers

The choice of wood and oakum was not simply a case of nostalgia. Materials were always a relatively small part of the equation in

previous page It didn't take much persuasion for Norwegian sailors to rally around their old boats. Sailing everything from the noble Colin Archer lifeboats to the ubiquitous "skerrycruisers", they converged on the festival at Risør as if they had never been away.

above What could be more natural than to sail Tasmania's unspoilt waters on a locally built wooden boat? The delightful 24ft (7.3m) *Madoc*, built of celery top and spotted gum, formed part of the Australian renaissance in the late 1980s.

right Constitution Dock, from which many of the great explorers set sail for Antartica, now once again plays host to a great variety of traditional craft. The Australian Wooden Boat Festival has been based there since the mid-1990s.

traditional boatbuilding. Dreamers with time on their hands could build a new wooden boat for less than the cost of a fibreglass one. And this was certainly a consideration behind one of the most famous wooden boat success stories of all time.

American Larry Pardey was another boat junkie with big dreams and a small wallet when he fell for a traditional-looking bermudan cutter, *Renegade*, drawn by Californian designer Lyle Hess back in the 1940s. She was based on the lines of those timeless British South Coast working boats, albeit with increased beam and a more yachtified wineglass shape underwater. While *Renegade's* design was ahead of her time, Pardey persuaded Hess to update it a little for him and set about building his dream boat. Pardey was soon joined by his partner Lin, who was just as much of a perfectionist as he was, and the two launched the immaculately-finished *Seraffyn* in 1968.

Thanks in large part to their prolific writing for magazines the world over, the couple's 11-year circumnavigation on the 7.3m (24ft) yacht made them almost household names among boating folk. What set them apart from most high-profile cruising sailors of that era, however, was not only that their boat was a wooden classic but that they sailed everywhere without an engine. The Pardeys' uncompromising example spawned a whole fleet of wooden cutters

to the same design, and soon the Sam L Morse Company in California was churning out a similar Hess design, ironically, in fibreglass…

In 1984 an 8.8m (29ft) version followed, called *Taliesin*, built to equally high standards and still without an engine, in which the Pardeys have to date sailed more than 65,000 miles, and still counting. Who said classic yachts were just made for sitting on the dock?

Saturated epoxy

It's quite likely that new wooden boats would have remained the slightly quirky province of the committed few had it not been for a major technological innovation that transformed the face of boatbuilding in the 1960s and '70s. When epoxy first appeared it was billed as a miracle glue that could bond a variety of different materials with enormous strength. Already widely used by pattern makers, it soon became clear that it held great potential for the marine industry. Athough boatbuilders had been experimenting with epoxy since the mid-1950s, it was the American Gougeon brothers who saw its potential for marine use. One of their main innovations was to adapt the glue so that it could be used as a coating to seal wood and fibreglass surfaces, an incredibly useful capability for boats. By 1971 Meade and Jan Gougeon had developed a comprehensive boatbuilding method which they marketed as the WEST (Wood Epoxy Saturation Technique) System.

Essentially, what the new system allowed was for a hull to be built using either strips or veneers of wood, moulded around a male plug and bonded together with epoxy. Typically, a large hull might be built of four layers of veneers, the centre two running diagonally at 90 degrees to each other and the inside and outside layers running fore-and-aft. The whole lot would then be coated with liquid epoxy. The result was an extremely water-resistant, monocoque hull that needed minimal internal bracing in the way of frames or floors, and was also considerably lighter than a conventional wooden hull. It was an ideal system for building one-off hulls where the cost of making a mould prohibited the use of fibreglass.

The Gougeon brothers initially used the technique to build a range of iceboats, although they soon realized that there was more money to be made from selling their epoxy to other builders than from building boats themselves. The first boat to be built using the WEST System was the 10.7m (35ft) trimaran Adagio, launched in 1970, and a long line of successful racing boats followed.

One of the first to embrace this new method of building was a young, up-and-coming American designer called Bruce King. Only three years after the Gougeons' own boat was launched, King used the WEST System to build a 12.5m (41ft) bermudan ketch for himself called *Unicorn*.

Ticonderoga and Whitehawk

King next applied the principle to one of Herreshoff's greatest designs, the legendary *Ticonderoga*, affectionately know as "Big Ti". He broadly kept the above-water profile of the yacht – albeit elongated from 22m to 28m (72-92ft) – added a daggerboard, and again built the hull using the WEST System. When *Whitehawk* was launched in 1978, she was the biggest boat in the world built in wood/epoxy. The rig was similarly updated to include electric winches and modern sail furling systems – although at 1210m² (13,000sqft) it looked every bit as impressive as the original and was said to push the yacht along at up to 16 knots.

To some, such tampering with a great master designer's work was tantamount to sacrilege and *Whitehawk* was not always looked upon with the affection that her fine lines deserved. Both *Unicorn* and *Whitehawk*, however, played an important role in bringing classic yacht design and construction into the late 20th century and, ultimately, ensured that this type of boat had a future.

But it wasn't just new-builds that were coming into the limelight. By the mid-1980s, the idea was beginning to catch on that some of the older boats might be restored, not as pseudo-modern yachts, with big doghouses and angular chrome windows, but as vintage craft. In the UK, the British J-Class *Velsheda* was rescued from a mud berth on England's south coast Hamble River and given a minimal refit before being chartered locally, while in the US the exquisite Fife cutter *Hallowe'en* began a five-year rebuild at the Museum of Yachting in Newport, Rhode Island.

From wreck to Olympic icon

One particularly symbolic early restoration took place in California. *Angelita* was an 8-Metre created by the American West Coast designer Nick Potter in 1930, winner of her class at the 1932 Olympics in Los Angeles – the first ever US gold medal in yacht racing. Not surprising, then, that she held a special place in US sailing history.

By the early 1980s, however, *Angelita* was virtually a wreck and was discovered just in time by a Santa Cruz syndicate who had her restored as the flagship of the 1984 Summer Olympics at Los Angeles. In a move that would have appalled her European counterparts, but which was quite common in the US, her hull was sheathed with three layers of Douglas fir all bonded together with epoxy. And, because her original designer had specified that all his drawings be burned after his death, there was little documentary evidence to base the restoration work on. Despite the inevitable compromises which resulted, *Angelita* played an important part in showing that there was a yachting heritage worth preserving and that there were people out there willing to invest time and money in doing so. It was now up to builders and owners to discover the best means to bring these old boats back to life in a manner most sympathetic to the original spirit of the craft.

in Search of Authenticity

Altair's appearance on the classic yacht scene had widespread repercussions. Acclaimed as one of the most authentic restorations undertaken, she was heralded by aficionados as an example of a new approach to yacht restoration, and the techniques adopted by her restorers, Southampton Yacht Services (SYS), were soon being emulated in yards around the world. By setting new levels of craftsmanship and authenticity, her restoration showed what was possible and set the standards that would prevail for the next 15 years. In a sense, the classic yacht world as we now know it began the day that *Altair* took to the water again.

left Although the rig configuration on the restored 8-Metre *Esterel* is original, a few concessions to modernity, such as synthetic sail cloth and ropes, mean she can now be raced harder than ever. The Côte d'Azur is now her playground.

On 8 July 1987 the 120ft (36.5m) schooner *Altair* was relaunched at Southampton, England, after an extensive two-year restoration. Apart from a few discreet concessions to modern technology, she looked much the same as she would have when she was launched by the Fife yard in Fairlie 56 years before. From her teak planking on oak frames and galvanized steel floors, to her lofty, off-white, gaff mainsail, the schooner had been lovingly refurbished to her original configuration. True, a layer of plywood had been added under the teak deck and modern electronics were concealed behind some of the wooden panelling below decks, but in most details she was true to the original.

Meyer's chance

Two years later, in Holland, another event of momentous significance for the yachting world took place. On 22 June 1989 the J-Class yacht *Endeavour* was craned into the water at the Royal Huisman Shipyard in Vollenhove, before being towed down the canal to the sea and sailed again for the first time in 52 years. *Endeavour* represented the first of Tom Sopwith's challenges for the America's Cup, in 1934, and the closest Britain ever came to lifting "the auld mug". The relaunching of "the darling jade" would have widespread repercussions, yet the story of her return to life was marked more by chance and circumstance than any conscious attempt to change the world.

When she visited Southampton in 1984, Elizabeth Meyer, wealthy granddaughter of an American newspaper owner, had no intention of owning a J-Class yacht. "I was there to write an article on J-Boats," she later told *Classic Boat* magazine. "I did not imagine in my wildest nightmares I would buy one." During the course of her research, however, Meyer came across the forlorn hull of the old racing yacht on a slip at Calshot, at the entrance to Southampton Waters where an attempt was being made by her young (but penniless owner) to restore her to Lloyd's A1. It was the beginning of a love affair that would see Meyer devote five years of her life – and millions of dollars – to restoring the boat and would ultimately lead to nothing less than the revival of the entire J-Class.

First, however, she had to get what remained of *Endeavour* to a shipyard. The hull was so far gone that it would have been dangerous to move it right away, so Meyer had a shed erected over her hull and hired a team of welders to make it safe. Endeavour was launched some months later and, after ballasting and some basic work to prepare her for the journey, towed to Holland. There she was craned onto a barge to be taken up to the Royal Huisman Shipyard at Vollenhove off the IJsselmeer – the vessel's 15ft 8in (4.8m) draught made it impossible to tow her up on her own keel. Royal Huisman had a reputation for building yachts to uncompromising standards and, under the guidance of Dutch designer Gerard Dijkstra, they pulled out all the stops for this prestigious project.

Unlike *Altair*, this was not going to be a purist restoration. Much was upgraded to modern standards. The rig was modernized and she was fitted with up-to-date amenities below decks. *Endeavour*'s headsails were bigger than in 1934 and, although the sail area remained unchanged, the mainsail was taller and narrower than the original to allow for a permanent backstay – at 165ft (50m), the new mast was said to then be the tallest in the world. The deck layout was laid out for modern winches and sheet tracks, as well as a small forest of ventilation cowls and deck prisms. Radar, satellite navigation, weatherfax, telex, watermakers, generators, hot water boilers, and a bow thruster completed the "technical upgrade" of the yacht below decks. *Endeavour* had all the trappings of a superyacht.

By the time the yacht was launched, Meyer had spent a rumoured $9.5 million on the restoration – paid for, no doubt, by her inheritance from the sale of the *Washington Post*, once owned by her grandfather. To put that investment into perspective, a fully-restored J is nowadays worth in the region of $25 million, while *Endeavour*'s current owner, ex-Tyco chairman L Dennis Kozlowski, spends around $700,000 a year just keeping the yacht running.

The yacht created a sensation when she returned to the Solent in 1989. There was simply nothing else like her around. Of the other J-Boats, *Velsheda* was still sailing, but by comparison looked drab and down at heel, while *Shamrock V* had long since been converted for cruising and was almost unrecognizable with her high bulwarks and bulky cabins. There were a few modern yachts that looked almost as flash, but nothing came close to matching the extreme hull shapes that characterized the J-Class. What's more, despite her modern accoutrements, and the fact that just a tiny amount of her original structure survived, *Endeavour* still had an undeniable sense of history about her and, wherever she went she was justifiably the star of the show.

Old Fifes restored

Meanwhile, the repercussions of the *Altair* restoration were continuing to be felt. For, apart from becoming a standard bearer for the cause of authenticity, *Altair* had brought together a team of craftsmen – including one Duncan Walker – who would go on to produce a series of outstanding restorations. Having shrewdly seen the way the wind was blowing, Walker had bought several derelict Fife hulls and, in 1990 formed Fairlie Restorations on the Hamble River with the express purpose of restoring yachts designed by the great William Fife III.

The new yard got off to a flying start with a project that would have almost as much impact as *Endeavour* and *Altair*. Built for the Duke of Medinacelli to compete against King Alphonso's *Hispania*, *Tuiga* was one of Fife's masterpieces. Like many of her ilk, however, the 15-Metre had been converted for cruising by the addition of ungainly cabins and a cut-down rig. On behalf of *Altair*'s owner Albert Obrist, Walker acquired her in a dilapidated state in Cyprus and sailed her back to the UK, almost sinking in the process. Over the next three years the yacht was completely rebuilt; from stem to stern, and from keel to mast truck. The result was another startlingly authentic restoration, from the scrubbed yellow pine decks (admittedly laid over plywood) to the hand-stitched Ratsey & Lapthorn sails. That almost nothing remained of the original boat may have worried some, but most were simply awed by the meticulous attention to detail.

But what really blew everyone away when *Tuiga* made her first appearance on the South of France classics scene at the Nioulargue regatta in 1993 was the sheer beauty of Fife's design. Up until then, the nearest anyone had seen to a gaff-rigged 15-Metre was a 12-Metre, which was beautiful enough, but the 15-Metres had always been more extreme, and *Tuiga* was no exception. With her low sheer and acres of sail – her boom alone was 56ft (17m) long – she was in a league apart.

It happened that the weather for the Nioulargue was particularly breezy that year and the photographers particularly snappy as *Tuiga* burst onto the scene in an explosion of spray, her cream-coloured sails scraping

previous page Another defining restoration of the 1980s was the J-Class yacht *Endeavour*. The American heiress Elizabeth Meyer sparked a trend for ever-larger classic yachts when she had the ex-America's Cup challenger rebuilt at the famous Royal Huisman shipyard in Holland.

above Getting to the guts of the problem. What started off as a refit ended up as a rebuild, as a new interior was built, the deckbeams were replaced, and a new stem fitted to the 1912 Fife schooner *Elise*. It's a common phenomenon with old wooden boats.

right Widely regarded as one of the most beautiful yachts on the Mediterranean circuit, the 1909 William Fife 15-Metre class cutter *Tuiga* was quickly snapped up by the prestigious Monaco Yacht Club following her restoration in 1993.

left Established in 1980 , the Gannon & Benjamin boatyard is one of the most prolific builders of wooden boats in the United States. When the 65ft (19.5m) *Juno* was launched, she was the largest boat built on Martha's Vineyard for over a century.

the waves. Some of the best-known modern images of classic yachts were photographed at the 1993 Nioulargue and ensured that the first 15-Metre to be restored remained etched in everyone's consciousness.

Altair and *Tuiga* set off a series of high-profile restorations in Europe, most of them destined to parade on the fashionable Mediterranean circuit. In Italy, yards such as Beconcini Cantiere Navale and the Cantieri Navali di la Spezia both in La Spezia had established a reputation for superior craftsmanship over the years and were the first port of call for owners with restoration projects. An indication of how attitudes had moved on was the increasing number of yachts that had been given makeovers in the 1970s and '80s and were now being brought back to the slipways to be given more sympathetic restorations. One such was *Mariette*, the last big Herreshoff schooner to survive, which returned to Beconcini's in 1994 having undergone a major rebuild at the yard just 12 years before. Her new owner, American entrepreneur Tom Perkins, had a new rig installed, returning the yacht to her original sail plan, with spars built by Harry Spencer in Cowes, on the Isle of Wight, and sails hand-stitched by that other great Cowes institution, Ratsey & Lapthorn. Some 150 of Herreshoff's original drawings were sourced from the Hart collection at the Massachusetts Institute of Technology (MIT) to ensure the vessel was as true to the original as possible.

American revival

On the other side of the Atlantic, the tendency seemed to be towards new-builds rather than major restorations. Take, for example, Gannon & Benjamin (G&B) in Martha's Vineyard, which had specialized in building small tenders and dayboats, and started receiving commissions for larger vessels. G&B's first big order was the 44ft (13.4m) *Liberty*, a traditionally-built gaff sloop that was launched in September 1986. Soon, there seemed to be no stopping the flow of yachts coming out of the yard: *Liberty* was followed by a 44ft schooner which, in turn, was followed by a 33ft (10m) ketch – both built of solid timber. Disaster struck in 1989, however, when the entire yard was burnt down by a freak fire. The astonishing community effort to rebuild it was testament to what an integral part of the society the yard had become in the 10 years since it was founded. Within a few months Gannon & Benjamin was back in business.

One of the yard's most significant restorations was the 63ft (19.2m) *When and If*. The 1938 Alden schooner was built in Maine for General George S Patton who intended to sail around the world on her, "when and if" he returned from World War II. In the event, Patton was killed in a car crash in Germany in 1945 and never fulfilled his dream. The yacht was sailed by the Patton family until the 1970s when she was donated to the Landmark School, near Boston, Massachusetts where she became a much-loved part of a sail-training programme for dyslexic

children. Then in 1990 she broke loose from her mooring during a gale and was wrecked just north of Boston. Although condemned as a total loss by her insurers, *When and If* was salvaged and carried by barge to Martha's Vineyard. There she was painstakingly restored by Gannon & Benjamin before finally being relaunched in June 1994. Since then, the schooner has become a familiar sight at most of the East Coast classic yacht events and has come to symbolize the survival of what was once thought to be a dying breed.

Another great survivor from the American East Coast was the 53ft (16.1m) Herreshoff cutter *Neith*. Built in 1907, she was much written up in the yachting press after crossing the Atlantic in 1920 – a feat rarely undertaken in those days in such a small craft. The yacht survived several near-disasters, including a sinking on the Connecticut River, before she was restored – twice – in the 1980s. Her second restoration, by Jack Brown, with the help of the Herreshoff Marine Museum in Bristol, Rhode Island, was the most comprehensive and included fitting a new interior, based on the original design, along with new deck houses and rigging. Jack's son Van Brown states that, "It is one of our goals to prove that a classic can be raced and cruised hard and still look beautiful". Her performance on the water against veteran as well as modern racing yachts has proven that point and helped raise the profile of classic yachts in general, as *Neith* once again became a darling of the media.

Small but perfect

Back in Scandinavia, the revival was taking a somewhat different turn. With a wealth of wooden boats having – despite the odds – survived the move to fibreglass, there were more beautiful old craft available than there were owners willing to restore them. Local experts speculate that the reason for this may be that Scandinavia was not ravaged by two world wars to the same extent as the rest of Europe. More prosaically, they also suggest, boats in this part of the world are usually taken out of the water during the winter months to prevent them being crushed by ice, giving owners ample opportunity to carry out vital maintenance work.

But while there was no shortage of smaller yachts, the tradition of building really big boats had never really taken off in Scandinavia so there were far fewer large classics around to restore – and hardly any that matched up to the glamorous Med starlets. While at a typical regatta in the South of France, a 12-Metre would have been regarded as medium-sized, in Norway it would have been the biggest boat there. And, unlike the rest of Europe, there were few major yards specializing in the restoration of classic yachts, because most boats were being restored, to varying degrees of competence, by their owners.

Trygve Barlag was one of the more extreme examples of dedicated ownership. Back in the early 1980s he found himself, the owner of a

above Another highly symbolic job taken on by Gannon & Benjamin was the restoration of the schooner *When & If*, which was wrecked off Boston. She has been described as "one of the finest historic vessels anywhere in the world".

right Classic yachts have many more strings to pull than modern boats, which is why they usually need bigger crews. Keeping it all neat and tidy, as on the immaculate 1929 Fife ketch *Belle Aventure*, is also a time-consuming business.

next page Built in 1907, the Herreshoff cutter *Neith* was almost consigned to a watery grave on the Connecticut River before being restored – twice – in the 1980s. She now successfully races in events such as the Eggemoggin Reach Regatta in Maine, USA.

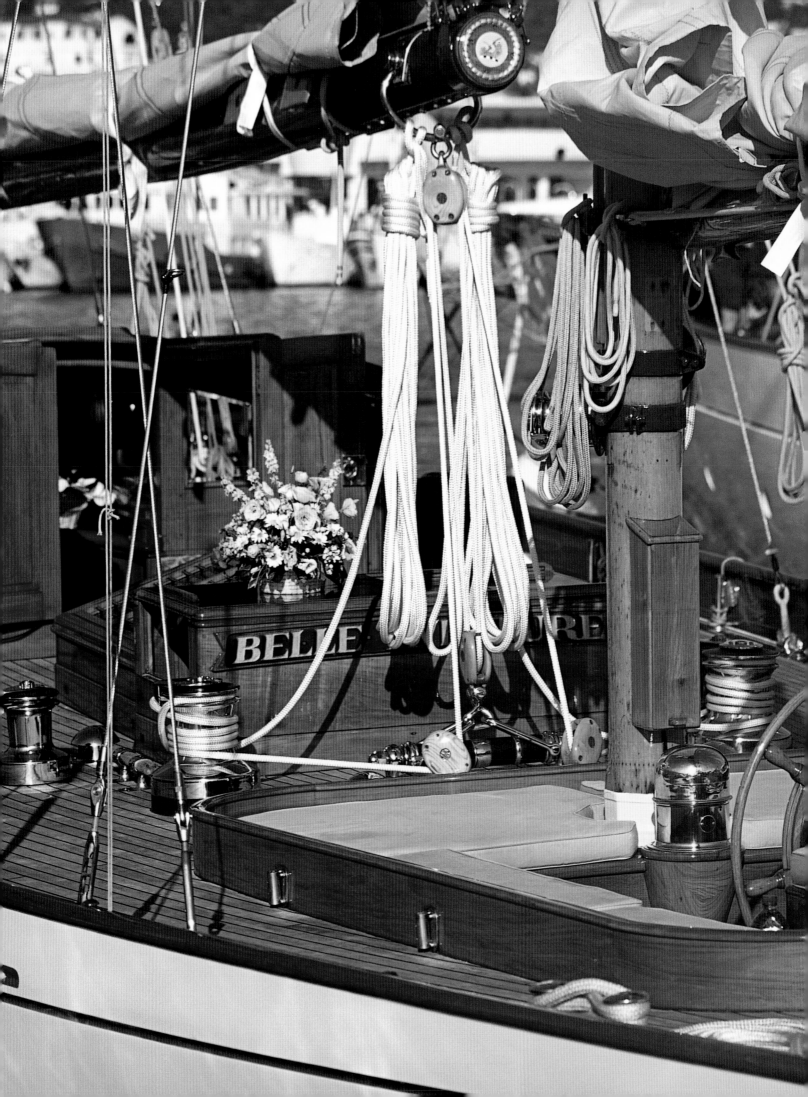

derelict wooden yacht. While looking through the small ads for a refrigerator, he spotted the remains of a boat called *Magnolia* for sale and went to have a look. The hull was a shambles and there was an internal waterline created after she had sunk at her moorings, but Barlag fell in love with the vessel's thrillingly long sheerline. After much haggling he eventually paid 8000 kroner (approx £800), not for the boat, he said, "but for the boat covers, on principle, as the hull had no value". The yacht itself was thrown in for free.

His instincts were absolutely spot on. What he had stumbled across was none other than the 12-Metre *Magda VIII*, renamed *Magnolia*, one of the craft owned by the renowned Norwegian sailor Alfred Larsen, and like all Larsen's boats she was of impeccable pedigree. Designed by William Fife in 1908, she was built by Anker & Jensen in Norway and had spent much of her life in Germany before eventually ending up back home forlorn and badly neglected.

It took Trygve 15 years to restore *Magnolia*, including replacing most of the planking, building new steel floors, and fitting an exquisite beech-panelled interior – in fact, the below-decks joinery took considerably longer to rebuild than the hull. During that time Trygve's life was turned upside down: he suffered a heart attack caused by too much stress, he was forced to sell his business, and, to cap it all, his marriage fell apart. For five years he was unable to work on the boat. By the time *Magnolia* was finally relaunched in the summer of 1999, Trygve had aged beyond his years but the boat looked almost the same as the day she was born.

By then the landscape of classic boat restoration had been transformed. Restoring old wooden boats was no longer just the province of the eccentric or the visionary but had become a highly specialized craft, practised by some of the top boatyards around the world. To the backyard tinkerers such as Trygve, who had grafted long and hard bringing their dishevelled hulks back to life, it must have seemed too good to be true. Whereas 20 years before they had been fighting a rearguard action against the seemingly inevitable onslaught of glassfibre, suddenly they were in the vanguard of a rapidly expanding movement.

A less arduous restoration was undertaken by German photographer Tom Nisch. He and his partner Angelika Berger had the good luck to stumble across Henry Rasmussen's own yacht *AR*, still in remarkably good shape despite having lead a full and interesting life. Drawn in 1935 to the German *seefahrtkreuser* class, she was the third yacht the legendary designer had designed for himself, but by 1981 was in the hands of a sailing school in Flensburg who wanted rid of her. Over the next few years, Tom and Angelika slowly replaced parts of the hull planking and had a whole new (butt-free) deck fitted by the Walsted yard in neighbouring Denmark. Unlike *Magnolia*, however, most of the original interior was in almost perfect condition

and only needed tidying up and rewiring. With her narrow beam and long overhangs (accounting for a third of her hull length), she once again became the epitome of German yachting elegance.

Australian extremes

As a result of Australia's largely inhospitable coast and extreme climate few old boats survived there, and those that did often seemed to be foreign yachts, abandoned by their owners midway through over-ambitious world voyages. Significantly, the oldest vessel in the country's maritime museum in Sydney is a yacht presented by the New Zealand government as a gift to the nation on Australia's 200th anniversary in 1988. *Akarana* was built 100 years earlier by Robert Logan's famous Kiwi yard to take part in the first centenary regattas in 1888. Like most New Zealand yachts the 62ft (18.9m) cutter had been extensively "modernized" – including alterations to her keel, rudder, and rig – but thanks to work undertaken since her move to Sydney, *Akarana* has been restored to her original configuration.

Significant developments were also taking place in the classics scene outside Sydney. Port Philip Bay, near Melbourne, is a 750-square mile "inland sea" and was the country's sailing capital until overtaken by Sydney. The principal port of Williamstown on its northern shore is home to Australia's oldest yacht club – the Royal Yacht Club of Victoria (RYCV) – and has been a base for several America's Cup challengers and Admiral's Cup teams. Port Philip Bay may no longer be the yachting mecca it once was but it has witnessed an astonishing revival of interest in classic yachts which is the envy of other parts of the country.

An anniversary restoration

In the late 1980s Hank Schilte, vice-commodore of the RYCV, spotted an old boat for sale in Sydney. Built in 1894 by Logan's, the 58ft (17.66m) *Waitangi* had been converted to a ketch rig and fitted out for cruising. Schilte formed a syndicate which bought the yacht and took her to Williamstown, Melbourne where they sailed her for several years. Then, as the 100th anniversary of her launch approached, they decided to restore the boat "to her former glory". The 13-month restoration was one of the most ambitious undertaken in Australia – some 3000 nails and 1500 screws were used to refasten the hull. Indeed, the timber structure of the triple-skinned, kauri hull had survived remarkably well and was left mostly untouched although, in a move that would now be regarded as sacrilege, it was sheathed with a layer of fibreglass to keep it watertight. Despite this small *faux pas*, *Waitangi* looked every bit as stunning when she was relaunched on 13 December 1994 as she must have done when she first touched water a century before.

1994 was also the year that the 1896 Camper & Nicholsons cutter *Avel* was re-launched on the South Coast of Britain following a long

previous page A labour of love is probably an understatement when describing Trygve Barlag's 15-year restoration of *Magnolia*. Although designed by William Fife III, the 12-Metre yacht was built by Anker & Jensen in Norway in 1908.

above That special inner glow. *Magnolia*'s exquisite panelled interior took longer to rebuild than everything else put together. The original joinery was damaged beyond repair after the yacht sank at her moorings in the 1970s.

right The restoration of the 1894 Logan cutter *Waitangi* in the early 1990s was a watershed for the classic yacht movement in Melbourne, Australia. Her hull was sheathed in glassfibre, accepted practice "down under" though frowned upon in Europe.

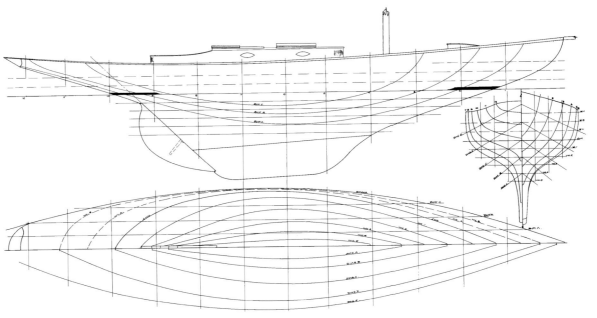

and detailed restoration at Harry Spencer's yard in Cowes, the Isle of Wight, and there are many similarities between these two 100-year-old yachts; their clipper bows, their wildly curvaceous hulls, their imposing gaff cutter rigs. But while *Avel* was immediately able to play among friends on the Med's lively classic yacht circuit, *Waitangi* was compelled to sail in splendid isolation. Not only was there nothing like her in Williamstown, but also there were very few yachts of her size and pedigree anywhere else in Australia.

Waitangi's restoration did, however, lend enormous impetus to the whole classic yacht movement in southern Australia. It led to the formation of the Classic Yacht Association of Australia in 1996 and the creation of a year-round season of classic yacht races named the Logan Series after their principal sponsor, the clothing manufacturer.

On the other side of the Tasman Sea in New Zealand the classic revival didn't really take hold until the 1990s, but this was mainly because most of the old boats had never gone away. Look out of the windows of the Royal New Zealand Yacht Squadron clubhouse at any point in the 1970s and '80s and you were likely to see a couple of veteran yachts milling among the modern fleet. The reason so many old boats had survived in New Zealand was largely because of the resilience of the triple-diagonal construction method pioneered by the country's top yards and combined with the durability of their beloved kauri – always the country's boatbuilding timber of choice. It also had much to do with the benign Kiwi climate: never too hot or too cold, and never too dry or too wet. Just what an old boat loves.

One by one the old boats had been converted for cruising. This usually meant the addition or extension of cabins and coachroofs and, since there was no prestige in having a clunky old gaff, being converted to bermudan rig. In some cases it even meant replacing the traditional keel-hung rudder with a modern skeg rudder. Chad Thompson, of the New Zealand Classic Yacht Association (NZCYA) estimates that by the early 1950s only three large yachts were still gaff-rigged.

Rona restored

One of the earliest and most ambitious projects undertaken was on New Zealand's South Island, where the 50ft (15.2m) *Rona* was exquisitely restored over a nine-year period. Designed by Scottish designer GL Watson and built by Robert Logan in 1893, the yacht had been fitted with a large doghouse, the end of her counter had been cut off, and her lead keel had been replaced by a large lump of concrete. Despite these obscenities, her owner John Palmer carefully pieced together the original elements of the old yacht, discovering a gooseneck fitting here, a trailboard there, until in August 1990 he relaunched one of the finest classics in the country.

But Palmer was ahead of his time and it wasn't until the early 1990s that the value of these old yachts came to be generally recognized.

left The Logans, New Zealand's most famous boatbuilding dynasty, designed sleek, low-slung yachts, well suited to the sheltered waters of Auckland's Waitemata Harbour. *Rawene* was no exception, as these lines demonstrate.

above The 42ft (12.6m) *Rawene* was built in 1908 for Auckland tailor Alf Gifford and owned by the same family for 95 years. After surviving 20 years in mothballs, she is thought to be the most original Logan afloat and is still winning races.

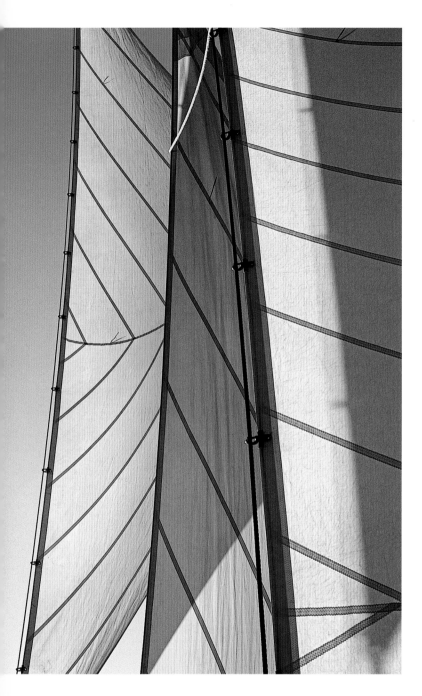

Ngataringa and Little Jim were two of the first boats to be restored to their original configuration, although both retained their "modern" aluminium spars. Then in the mid-1990s, the 1895 Bailey-built Thelma (known as "Little" Thelma in deference to the 59ft (18m) Logan cutter of the same name built in 1898) was converted back to gaff rig. Others soon followed suit and gradually more and more boats began reverting to their original appearance as they raised gaff sails for the first time in a generation. At the same time many shed their boxy cabins and wheelhouses in favour of their original open cockpits and sleek cabins. By 1995 the revival had gained enough momentum to warrant its own club, and that summer, in the richly-varnished interior of the 1923 Bailey-designed cutter Prize, the NZCYA was formed.

A Kiwi time capsule

One yacht that managed to remain largely unaltered throughout was the 1908 Logan cutter Rawene. The last large sailing yacht built by the Logan Bros before the yard closed in 1910, she was commissioned by Alf Gifford, who ran a successful tailoring business. Gifford raced the yacht unaltered for 40 years, by which time he was well into his 90s, before handing her over to his son Jack. It was Jack who, at the age of five, had swung the bottle at Rawene's launching and had learned to sail on her as "bow boy", eventually becoming an accomplished sailor in his own right. After a few years racing with friends, Jack realized that Rawene was becoming uncompetitive against her bermudan counterparts. Rather than alter her in any way, he decided to put her beyond the vagaries of fashion by storing her undercover at a nearby yard.

Although there were many who criticized this "waste" of a good yacht it was, in a way, a visionary act. For while the rest of the classics fleet was being chopped about in a futile attempt to keep up with the times, Rawene sat in her own time capsule for 20 years. By the time Jack was persuaded to relaunch her in 1979, she was acclaimed as the most original Logan in New Zealand and, after being loaned to the Brookes, a well-known Auckland sailing family, was eventually placed with the Auckland Maritime Museum in 1992. There she languished for a number of years, apparently beyond the capabilities of the museum, until Jack reclaimed her and entrusted her once again to the Brookes family. By then, the yacht's significance was fully appreciated and, after some minor repairs, she was smartened up and put back on a mooring opposite Jack Gifford's house in exactly the same spot where his father had kept her all those years before. From there, Rawene joined the rest of the classics fleet on their regular races, a unique incarnation of a great New Zealand boatbuilding tradition.

Marigold and Partridge

In the relatively short history of classic yacht restoration, two boats stand out above all others; not because they were especially

above It's all very well doing a nice restoration, but someone has to know how to handle those acres of sail once the boat's complete. Partridge's saviour Alex Laird has proven adept at both, sweeping the board clean on the Med circuit.

right An apprentice shipwright, Alex had to train himself in all aspects of boatbuilding – from keel-casting to wire-splicing – to restore Partridge. It took him 18 years. He tastes the fruit of his labours up aloft during a race off Cannes.

next page From a derelict hulk on the mud flats of Essex, the Camper & Nicholsons-built Partridge was reborn as one of the most admired classic yachts on the scene. She set sail again on the Solent in June 1998 for the first time in decades.

extravagant or lavish, but because they were both the culmination of years of work by two individuals striving, each in his own way, towards authenticity. Both boats are remarkable personal achievements as well being landmark restorations in their own right.

The modern-day story of *Marigold* starts the day sculptor Greg Powlesland spotted a derelict hull lying up a wooded creek on the Isle of Wight in 1981. It was the 1892 Nicholson-designed cutter *Marigold*, stripped of all her fittings and waiting to be turned into a houseboat. For Powlesland, the sight reawoke memories of a model – made by his father – which had captivated him as a child. Although he had no experience of boatbuilding, within a week Powlesland had bought the boat. It was eight years later that Powlesland finally admitted defeat and put the boat up for auction. Her unlikely buyer was Glen Allan, a regular International One-Design (IOD) racer who had never sailed on a classic yacht and bought the boat, sight unseen, on condition that Powlesland would supervise her restoration.

What followed was essentially a study in authenticity. The hull was reframed and replanked, and new floors and hanging knees cast in bronze; a solid teak deck was laid and caulked with cotton and payed with Jeffery's Marine Glue (ie, hot pitch) – no plywood or modern sealants here. Not content with merely returning the yacht to her original gaff cutter rig, Powlesland had a suit of cotton sails made by famed East Coast sailmaker James Lawrence of Brightlingsea, Essex and all the running rigging made of hemp or manila. Below decks, the mahogany panelling was set off by some elaborate scrollwork and the button upholstery was stuffed with horsehair.

above Keeping below decks as original as possible is just as important as above decks. The 32ft (9.6m) *Lona II* is a little jewel designed by amateur designer J Pain Clark in 1905 and luckily still in largely original condition.

left The Fife schooner *Elise* and the Camper & Nicholsons cutter *Marigold* catch the evening light on the Beaulieu River, UK. *Marigold* is probably the most authentic yacht restoration ever undertaken outside a museum – even down to her horsehair cushions!

next page The 60ft (18m) cutter *Avel* was built by Camper & Nicholsons for a French owner in 1896. She was "retired" in 1925 and used as a houseboat for 65 years before being restored in 1994. Here she is sailing off St Tropez soon after relaunch.

The only concessions to modernity were the waterproof bulkheads and additional knees required to satisfy the Lloyd's 100A1 regulations, and a small engine linked to a hydraulic transmission. Otherwise she was in almost every detail an accurate reconstruction of Nicholson's original design.

Marigold was relaunched on 7 April 1993 and the following year won the Hermès-Mumm trophy for classic yachts on the Solent, beating Eric Tabarly's classic Fife cutter *Pen Duick*. But, despite *Marigold*'s significance, this exceptional restoration – probably one of the most authentic ever undertaken – went by relatively unnoticed. Perhaps it was due to her owners' modest manner and their preference for an anonymous cruise to Norway to the glitz and hype of the Mediterranean regattas, which meant that *Marigold* didn't acquire the fame she deserves. Or perhaps she was ahead of her time.

No such problem with Alex Laird's protégée *Partridge*. There was even less left of the 50ft (15m) yacht when the apprentice boatbuilder spotted her elegant hull lying askew on the Essex mudflats in 1980. In fact, so little of her remained that no one even knew her name or provenance. It took some research before Laird discovered that she was called *Partridge*, and that she had been designed by J Beavor Webb (designer of the 1885 and 1886 British America's Cup challengers *Genesta* and *Galatea*) and built at Camper & Nicholson's in 1885. By pure chance – and an appreciative eye for a fine line – he had stumbled across a genuine thoroughbred.

It took Laird 10 years just to restore the hull, working mostly on his own, including casting the 10-tonne lead keel in his parents' garden. Like Powlesland, authenticity was his prime goal although, unlike Powlesland, Laird was prepared to use modern materials "when I felt they would have been used in 1885, had they been available". So, *Partridge* is fitted with a plywood subdeck; the deck is sealed using modern caulking compounds; and the sails and ropes are made of modern synthetic materials – albeit with period styling. Set against that, *Partridge* is authentic in every detail for a yacht of her period, from the shape of her cleats to the radius on a hatch corner. As well as researching from old books and photographs, Laird soon met up with Powlesland, and the pair exchanged useful information as well as giving each other much-needed moral support. In the later years, Laird was also able to draw on the example of the 1896 Camper & Nicholsons cutter *Avel*, also being restored on the Isle of Wight.

It took Laird 18 years to complete the task, but *Partridge* finally set sail again in May 1998 for the first time in several decades. The following year Laird took her down to the Med where, thanks partly to a rating which favoured her highly original restoration, she swept the board for her first couple of seasons. Her uncompromising restoration was certainly a factor in the increasingly purist attitudes that would come to prevail in the classic boat world.

Spreading
the Word

From its hesitant beginnings in the 1970s and '80s, by the end of the 1990s the classic yacht movement had established itself as a force to be reckoned with. But although the strength of the revival was now much less in doubt, the standard of quality was still variable. During the next decade, the high standards set by *Altair* would increasingly radiate out to revivalists around the world. And as the yachts' standing rose, so did their value. Soon, people would be referring to classic yachts as "collector's items" and "floating paintings".

left J-Class fever hit the sailing world in the 1990s, when all three surviving Js were reborn as superyachts. As well as being given a modern rig, the 1933 *Velsheda* (K7) had her hull reshaped and faired to improve her performance.

The stir created by *Endeavour* when she reappeared on the scene in 1989 ensured that, sooner or later, the other two surviving J-Class boats would be restored to a similar standard. First off was *Shamrock V*, the only one of the three to have been in continuous use since her construction in 1930 and the only one built of wood (the other two being steel). By then Meyer had become the acknowledged J expert and, while the work on her own yacht *Endeavour* was in the final phases, she oversaw the partial restoration of *Shamrock V* in Newport, Rhode Island – including lowering the bulwarks and deckhouses. *Velsheda* was next, although she underwent such a dramatic modernization at the hands of Dutch superyacht designer Gerard Dijkstra that by the time she was relaunched in September 1999, like *Endeavour*, she was essentially a new yacht.

Two years later, *Shamrock V* underwent her second, this time complete, restoration, and again Meyer was – initially at least – put in charge. But although it was only 12 years since *Endeavour* had been completed there had in that time, as Meyer herself realized, been a sea change in the ethos of classic yacht restoration. "The *Endeavour* restoration took place in a vacuum," Meyer later wrote. "No-one was restoring much of anything, and there were essentially no sailing yachts of her size, old or new, in commission. *Endeavour*'s styling includes elements of the [American] Js *Ranger* and *Yankee*, of the Phil Rhodes-designed CCA Maxi, *Escapade*, and of my Concordia yawl, *Matinicus*. *Shamrock V*, however, is a different story… *Shamrock V*'s present owner approached this restoration with very definite goals. He wanted his boat to be returned as near as possible to her 1930's look, while allowing for modern systems, better crew quarters and maximized sailing qualities."

Authentic restoration

This observation was symptomatic of how the classic yacht scene as a whole had developed. In the late 1980s a project on the scale of *Endeavour* was so radical that it was sufficient just to mimic the styling of the 1930s, but a decade later the issue of authenticity had acquired such central importance that yards were expected to replicate the minute detailing not just of a particular period, but of a particular vessel at a particular period. It was a seismic change in philosophy that had evolved virtually one boat at a time, becoming more and more refined as each restoration inspired the next, and as knowledge was spread from one restorer to the next.

At the forefront of this movement was Fairlie Restorations, the yard near Southampton, England that had rebuilt *Tuiga* to such stunning effect. Other prestigious restorations at Fairlie's soon followed: the 8-Metre *Fulmar* in 1994; the 85ft (26m) ketch *Kentra* in 1995; the 49ft (15m) cutter *Madrigal* in 1997, and another 15-Metre *The Lady Anne* in 1999; the 8-Metre *Siris* in 2000; and the Cork Harbour One-Design *Jap*

previous page One of California's most famous yachts, the 1935 *Santana* was owned by a string of celebrities including Humphrey Bogart. "Bogie" had a 12-year love affair with the Sparkman & Stephens schooner (then a yawl) and won several races on her.

in 2002. Fairlie's still has an impressive collection of old Fifes awaiting restoration, including that other *Tuiga*-in-waiting, the 15-Metre *Hispania*.

On the East Coast of America, several yards that had been pioneers of the wooden boat revival during the 1970s were now, 20 years on, reaping the rewards of their foresight and receiving commissions for large new-builds and rebuilds. And, as in Europe, many yachts that had been worked on in the 1980s were back for "reinterpretation". Among them was the 1932 Olympic Gold winning 8-Metre *Angelita*, symbol of Californian yachting pride – but this time her owners chose an Atlantic yard for her second restoration: the William Cannell Boatbuilding Co in Camden, Maine.

Soon after *Angelita* was relaunched, the Cannell yard was given charge of another Nick Potter-designed yacht the 62ft (18.9m) N-Class sloop *Serenade*, a dainty double-ender once owned by French marine biologist Jacques Cousteau and Hollywood film star Zsa Zsa Gabor (though not at the same time!). Once again, the yard had the problem of having almost no original drawings of the boat, but this time they were fortunate because *Serenade* had survived in remarkably original condition. Even her deck fittings – usually the first things to be modernized – nearly all dated back to the 1930s, from her original Herreshoff windlass to her original Herreshoff binnacle. Thus the yard had ample reference as they undertook the necessary strengthening work, including replacing all the frames, fitting a new deck, new

above left Although extensively rebuilt in 1997, *Santana*'s interior is much the same as was enjoyed by Lauren Bacall, Frank Sinatra, Ingrid Bergman, Richard Burton and David Niven in the 1940s and '50s. Even the bevelled glass doors are as per original.

above The interior of the 1930 J-Class yacht *Shamrock V* was considerably modified during restoration to take into account the new deck configuration. Proper bathrooms were among the additions, as befitted her new superyacht status.

right Originally restored as a flagship for the 1984 Olympics in Los Angeles, the Nick Potter 8-Metre *Angelita* was brought back to more original condition by the William Cannell boatyard in the 1990s. She's now as good as new.

next page *Serenade* makes the most of a breeze during the Eggemoggin Reach Regatta in Maine. The N-Class yacht was built for violinist Jascha Heifetz in 1938 and extensively rebuilt in 2000, though she remains largely original.

deckhouses, and new engine. Most of her planking, however, and her delightful Butternut panelled interior remained original.

Meanwhile, another celebrity yacht was being revived on the Pacific coast. Although owned by a string of Hollywood actors during the 1940s, '50s, and '60s, *Santana* will always be remembered as "Bogie's boat". Humphrey Bogart owned the 55ft (16.74m) yacht from 1945 until his death in 1957. Under Bogart's ownership, stars such as Ingrid Bergman, Richard Burton, David Niven, Frank Sinatra, and, of course, Lauren Bacall were all visitors on board *Santana*. Bogart not only sailed her on weekends but also won several races in her, most memorably the 1950 San Clemente Island Race and the 1952 Channel Islands Race off the coast of California. Designed in 1935 by Sparkman & Stephens as a schooner, she was converted to yawl in the early 1940s.

But time took its toll and eventually, in 1997, *Santana* sank at her mooring in San Francisco; it seemed as if her end was nigh. Paul and Chrissy Kaplan spotted her the following year and, despite being warned off such a major undertaking, decided to restore the yacht. The work was carried out by the KKMI boatyard in San Francisco and, while returning the boat to many of her original features such as the schooner rig, added several that were not entirely authentic, including a new fibreglass cockpit. Most controversially, perhaps, the bowsprit was built of carbon fibre and painted with a faux wood effect. Not only that, but also, instead of running through a hole in the bulwark, as is traditional, the inside end of the bowsprit was butted onto a stainless steel pivot fitted onto the stem. Clearly, the concept of authenticity so feverishly advocated in Europe had not quite reached California.

Despite these deviations, *Santana* made a spectacular sight when she was relaunched two years later. More than anything, it seemed, people were just happy to see the return of "Bogie's boat".

Italian passion

Back in Europe, an Italian yard was beginning to get a name for its outstanding restoration work. The Cantiere Navale dell'Argentario was originally established to service the fleet of fishing boats in Porto Santo Stefano in Tuscany. The decline of the fishing fleet forced the yard to look for work elsewhere, but rather than go down the production boat route it chose an area with which its traditional skills had some affinity: classic yachts. The arrival of a charismatic new managing director with a bulging contacts' book secured the yard's future direction. For Federico Nardi was not just out to save some old boats and find a little work for the yard, he was on a mission. These old boats, he argued, were far more than mere means of transport; they were works of art and they should be valued accordingly. "The boat is like a painting," said Nardi, "except it floats. And yet it costs much less than the paintings that many people around the world buy."

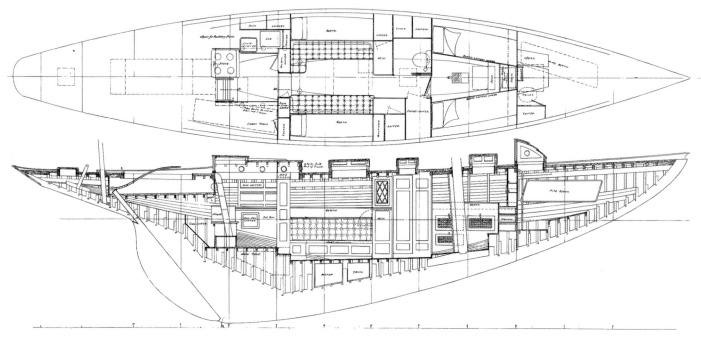

With this vision in mind, he set about convincing several wealthy patrons that they should invest some of their savings in acquiring these "floating paintings". The idea was not without precedence. Just as the Medici family had supported many of the great artists of the Renaissance, including Michelangelo, by commissioning their work, so the current aristocracy could now show their commitment to the nation's cultural heritage by commissioning fine yacht restorations. After all, if they didn't invest then these irreplaceable maritime artefacts might be lost forever. And if that investment meant they had to join the ranks of other high-society owners swanning around on their yachts in the Mediterranean, then that was a price worth paying too.

There was nothing new about yachts being used as status symbols – particularly among the stylish Italians, who had for many years coupled their passion for sailing with their love of display. Indeed, buying a classic was a way for the wealthy cognoscenti not only to show off their fabulous wealth but also to display their good taste, for while the rich and brash might buy the latest Wally or Oyster glassfibre and carbon fibre superyachts, the latter-day Medicis knew that real cultural kudos lay in buying a classic yacht.

The first wealthy patron to fall under Nardi's spell was his former sailing buddy Patrizio Bertelli, head of Prada and sponsor of Italy's 2003 America's Cup challenger in Auckland, *Luna Rossa*. After passing on two Fifes, *Belle Aventure* and *Altair*, Bertelli eventually agreed to take on a rather more racy American 12-Metre that Nardi had tracked down. This was Olin Stephens's *Nyala*, which, in 1938, established him as the pre-eminent designer of Twelves. Nardi bought the yacht for $120,000 and had her shipped back to the Cantiere Navale dell'Argentario. Here, all the underwater planking and all the frames

previous page The New York 30 Linnet is one of a growing collection of floating paintings restored by the Cantiere Navalle dell'Argentario in Porto Santo Stefano, Italy. She is one of several yachts owned by Prada boss and sailing enthusiast Patrizio Bertelli.

below *Dorade*'s strong but light construction meant she could hold her sail for longer than most. Stephens recalls that during her victorious Fastnet race, "we carried full sail when the rest of the fleet reefed, many deeply, and some were hove-to".

above left Old blends almost imperceptibly with new in *Dorade*'s newly restored interior. Designed for racing, the accommodation is practical rather than commodious, with ample storage in the mahogany panelled lockers.

left Designed when Olin Stephens was just 21, *Dorade* launched a new breed of ocean racing yachts. Not dissimilar to the "Metre" yachts, she carried all her ballast in her keel and was more lightly built than most ocean racers of her era.

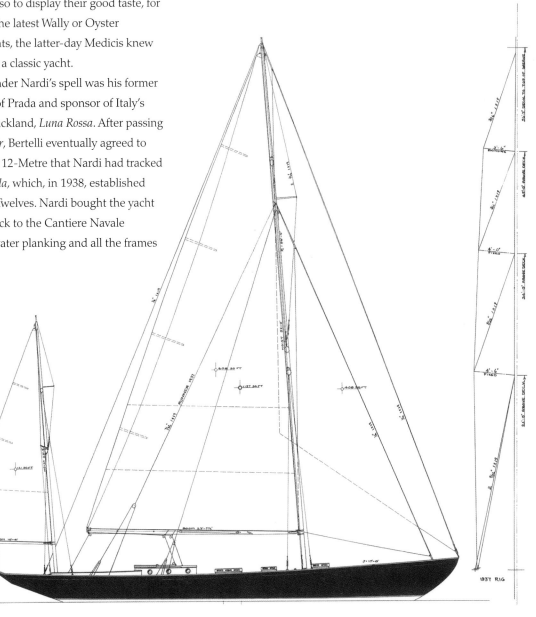

were replaced, along with all the deck and deckbeams. The yard's quality of workmanship and passionate attention to historical detail ensured that when *Nyala* was refloated in 1995 she was one of the most outstanding yachts on the Mediterranean circuit.

Nyala not only catapulted the Cantiere Navale dell'Argentario firmly into the classics arena but she also started the yard's seeming obsession with yachts by American designers and, in particular, with that seminal designer Olin Stephens. Apart from cultural and aesthetic preferences, there were some purely pragmatic reasons for this bias. "We avoid boats with galvanized metal structures inside, and many of the European boats are like that," Nardi explained, with reference to the steel floors and fastenings of many yachts built in Europe before World War II, which often become corroded and damage the boat's structure. "American boats are also cheaper," he observed.

Ironically, yards such as Nardi's had to some extent become victims of their own success and the price of even the most dilapidated old boat, providing it had the right designer's name attached, soared. So collectors were beginning to look further afield for affordable projects to take on. It's an indication of how much more highly valued these yachts were in Europe that so many of America's most famous craft were being snapped up by Europeans and taken across the Atlantic for restoration.

An all-American great

A case in point was the Cantiere Navale dell'Argentario's next project. The 1930 yawl *Dorade* holds a special place in the pantheon of historic craft as the yacht that heralded the arrival of America's (and arguably the world's) greatest living designer. Olin Stephens designed the boat when he was just 21 years old and her wins in the 1931 and 1932 Fastnet Races brought the newly-formed partnership of Sparkman & Stephens recognition worldwide. With Olin installed as chief designer, the company would go on to become one of the biggest names in the history of yachting.

Dorade went on to win many more races, mainly based in the US, but eventually in the mid-1990s her then owner, Michael Douglas, decided to put her up for sale. Realizing the significance of the vessel, he was keen to find a buyer who would keep her in America. He searched in vain. "When I listed the boat," Douglas told *Wooden Boat* magazine, "I actually specified a higher price if she were to go overseas. I think it's a shame *Dorade* is not here in the United States. The bad news is we've lost a piece of American history. The good news is they did an absolutely wonderful job of restoring her…"

For Nardi, the agreed price of just over $100,000 was a bargain for a yacht of *Dorade*'s pedigree. His client this time was Pirelli director Giuseppe Gazzoni Frascara, whose other sporting interests include ownership of the Bologna football club. A $400,000 restoration

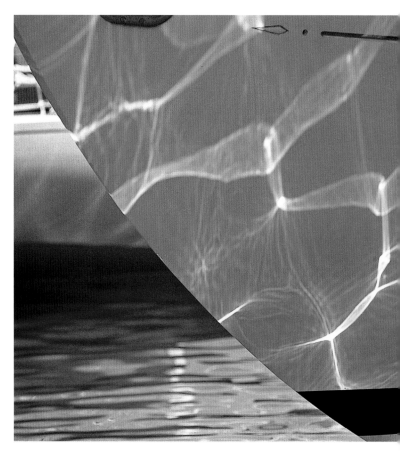

above Reflections play on the bows of *Stormy Weather* after her relaunch at the Cantiere Navale dell'Angentario. She was the third Sparkman & Stephens yacht restored by the yard and was followed by the S&S cutter *Sonny*.

right A very 21st century blend of old and new. While the wooden blocks look traditional enough, they often conceal a modern mechanism which help them run more freely, and the multiplat cordage clearly doesn't date from the 1930s.

next page Masthead view of the 1935 Fastnet winner *Stormy Weather* the day after she was relaunched following a "50 per cent rebuild" in Italy. Her designer Olin Stephens sits besides the mizzen of what is said to be his favourite offspring.

followed, including replanking the underwater hull, fitting a new teak deck, and replacing the wheel steering with a tiller. *Dorade*'s relaunch in June 1997 was attended by her designer, by then 89 years old. It was the start of a close personal relationship between the American grand master and the Italian cantiere.

Nyala and *Dorade* were soon joined by a fleet of equally esoteric yachts, mostly American, restored to the same impeccable standard. They included the Herreshoff-designed New York 30 *Linnet*, a second commission for Prada boss Bertelli, and two other famous Olin Stephens designs – the 1935 Fastnet winner *Stormy Weather*, and the 1935 cutter *Sonny*, restored in 2001 and 2002 respectively. Non-American projects included the 1938 Laurent Giles cutter *Cerida*, and, more recently, the 1899 Charles Sibbick fin-keeler *Bona Fide*.

It was nothing less than a renaissance of Italian classic yachting, and other prominent figures were soon starting to make regular visits to Nardi's crammed office overlooking the busy boatyard in Porto Santo Stefano. The America's Cup designer Doug Peterson brought his own classic yacht *Tamara IX*, a largely original 12-Metre designed by Anker & Jensen, which underwent a gradual restoration. Another famous visitor and personal friend of Nardi's was the Argentinian designer Germán Frers who had his distinctive 1909 Nicholson-designed 8-Metre *Folly* shipped all the way from his homeland to be rerigged by the yard before joining the racing circuit.

It was a fertile blend of old and new; of venerable old masters mixing it with cutting-edge contemporary designers, all brought together in a traditional boatyard working on some of the most graceful yachts in the world. No wonder Italy's cognoscenti fell in love with classic yachts all over again.

A precocious talent

The Norwegian revival found its most enthusiastic proponent in a young man who only a few years earlier might have been learning his times tables rather than spearheading a wooden boat revival. When it came to old boats, however, Peter Ennals had always been the young man in a hurry. By the age of 12 he was buying and selling dinghies, and had already restored his first boat. Within a few years he had traded up to a 10-Metre, which also underwent a complete rebuild, and, aged 16, he formed the Norwegian Classic Yacht Club. That was in 1990, and five years later Ennals set up one of Norway's first wooden boatbuilding schools on a derelict site outside Oslo. The school received two million kroner (approx £155,000) of state funding in its first year and developed into something of a mecca for young wooden boat enthusiasts. By the time he established the European Classic Yacht Union in 1996, this precocious young boating enthusiast was one of the central figures in Scandinavia's burgeoning classic boat scene.

left When not designing state-of-the-art America's Cup yachts and luxury cruising yachts, Argentinian designer Germán Frers likes to play on his 1909 Nicholson 8-Metre *Folly*, here seen chasing the Laurent Giles *Cerida* off Porto Santo Stefano in Italy.

above One of the innovations devised by Rod and Olin Stephens was the dorade air vent, so-called after the yacht for which it was first designed, the double Fastnet winner *Dorade*. The modern substitute is rather more complicated: air conditioning.

But Ennals's great love was for the Metre yachts and, in particular, the largest of the type to survive in Norway: the 12-Metres. Although there were several still sailing in somewhat dilapidated condition, or converted to cruising, there was almost nothing in Scandinavia to compare to the glittering Twelves on the Mediterranean circuit. That was all to change in 1998, when the 12-Metre *Erna Signe* was brought to Norway for restoration. Designed by William Fife III but built at the Swedish capital, Stockholm, the yacht won silver in the 1912 Olympics and, after a chequered history, which included being requisitioned by the Nazis, ended up in France. Ennals was closely involved with tracking the yacht down on behalf of the Schrøder family, descendants of the original Norwegian owner, and having her shipped to the Walsted yard in Denmark for complete restoration.

In truth, Walsted's was one of the few yards in Scandinavia capable of taking on a project of this scale. Founded in 1949 by Aage Walsted, the yard was responsible for a late flourish of wooden yachts in the 1950s and '60s, with designs by the likes of Dane Aage Nielsen and Sparkman & Stephens, which earned them a well-deserved reputation for fine craftsmanship. After surviving the 1970s and '80s by fitting out fibreglass hulls (the hulls themselves were built elsewhere), they turned their attention to yacht restoration in the 1990s, taking on such projects as the 1919 Anker & Jensen 12-Metre *Thea* and the magnificent 1879 former German revenue cutter *Kong Bele* (ex-*Dryaden*).

No expense was spared to restore *Erna Signe*, including returning the hull to the original varnish and fitting a gaff cutter rig, as it would have been in 1912. With her brushed stainless steel fittings and all-varnish deck joinery, *Erna Signe* was completely outstanding when she finally returned to Norway in 2000. And this time Ennals was on board not just as project manager but as skipper.

Erna Signe was soon joined by another 12-Metre, restored alongside her during her final year at Walsted's: the 1933 *Vema III*, built by Anker & Jensen in Norway. Her restoration was the culmination of 20 years' hard slog by her owner Tor Jørgen Dahl, which saw him finally give up most of his share in the boat in order to have her professionally restored and kept in Norway. In a matter of months Walsted had completed the work Dahl had been struggling to do for half his adult life and, to his evident satisfaction, *Vema III* went on to win the prize for Best Professionally Restored Yacht at Norway's Risør Wooden Boat Festival in 2000.

Even yachts that were still in full commission were not beyond improvement. The popular 1938 Jensen-designed 12-Metre *Eileen*, which had been continuously sailed in Norwegian waters for the best part of 60 years, was snapped up by a Dutch owner and taken to the Van Noort yard in Holland, who were already in the process of restoring the Anker 8-Metre *Varg III*, for a little "purification". What was billed as a refit turned into more of a rebuild, when parts of

Eileen's hull and deck had to be replaced and the rig was returned to its original configuration.

On the other side of the world, great things were continuing to happen in Port Phillip, near Melbourne, Australia. One of the key players in the successful *Waitangi* syndicate had been Col Anderson, a well-known local yachtsman, winner of two Sydney-to-Hobart races as well as an Admiral's Cup, who owned the Hood sail loft in Melbourne. Soon after *Waitangi* was launched, he started work on his own project, a 50ft (15m) gaff cutter drawn by Australian designer Charlie Peel and launched in 1923. *Acrospire III*, or "Little Ack" as she was known, was a sylph compared to the full-bodied Logan cutter *Waitangi*, but her uncompromising restoration showed what could be done with a great deal of care and thought rather than bucketloads of cash, and helped raise the game a little bit further.

A daunting task

By the time the Melbourne group came to their third major project, they had 10 years' experience sailing and restoring classic yachts and their skills had developed accordingly. It was just as well because their next task was somewhat daunting. For nearly a century Australia's yachtsmen had competed for the privilege of raising the famous Sayonara Cup, but what was perhaps less well known was that the yacht after which the cup was named was still afloat, albeit in a poor state of repair, in Sydney Harbour. The legendary 57ft 7in (17.6m) gaffer, designed by William Fife III and built in Adelaide in 1897, had been the pride of Melbourne after she beat the Royal Sydney Yacht Squadron's "unbeatable" contender, *Bona*, in a one-to-one challenge in 1904. Despite her high standing in Melbourne, however, she was subsequently sold to Sydney where she has remained ever since.

Anderson and Doug Shields, another *Waitangi* mover and shaker, tracked the boat down and formed another syndicate to buy her and bring her back to Melbourne for restoration. This time there were no half-measures and *Sayonara* was almost entirely rebuilt, including completely reframing and refastening the hull, and fitting a new deck, interior, and rig. By the time she was relaunched in May 2000, the hull planking was about all that was left of the original, and that had been traditionally caulked and sealed. No fibreglass sheathing this time.

The return of *Sayonara* to Port Phillip Bay was a capping triumph for the Melbourne group headed by Anderson and Shields who, in less than 10 years, had formed the nucleus of a movement almost in isolation. It also marked a significant step forward from the work undertaken on *Waitangi* just six years before. Elsewhere, the ethical approach to rebuilding these venerable old craft was constantly evolving and seemingly moving towards ever-greater authenticity.

Another Australian restoration that put originality to the fore was the 38ft (11.6m) *Aorere*. Built at St Kilda, near Melbourne in 1898 to

left Another Anker & Jensen creation, the 1938 12-Metre *Eileen*, was taken to Holland for restoration. Her concours standard finish was soon being exhibited along with other like-spirited yachts on the fashionable Mediterranean circuit.

above A close-up view of the fine craft of traditional sailmaking. Although the seams are machine stitched, most of the detail work such as the leathering and slide lashings have to be done by hand – fiddly and time-consuming work.

very similar lines as a Logan yacht of the same name, she ended up in Western Australia in the mid-1980s after a typically mixed life. Although stripped out and re-timbered in the early 1990s, her restoration proper didn't start until 1995. Which was probably just as well because, by then, her new owners had become well-versed in the concept of classic yacht restoration. As a result, they avoided modern materials wherever possible, and caulked the planking in traditional style with cotton, payed with white lead on the hull and Jeffrey's Marine Glue on the deck. Copper and bronze fastenings were used throughout and stainless steel was avoided wherever possible.

It's an approach that few would have advocated 10 years earlier but which suits the vessel's construction. By their very nature, wooden hulls have a tendency to "move" and anything that attempts to turn them into rigid modern structures is unsympathetic to that essential characteristic and is likely to cause problems. The few places where modern sealants and epoxies were used on *Aorere*, they have either leaked or starting showing hairline cracks, and have subsequently been replaced with white lead.

Also in the mid-1990s, yet another local hero was being brought back to life on Auckland's waterfront in neighbouring New Zealand. The restoration of the famous Tercell Brothers' cutter *Ranger* was one of the most thorough undertaken in the country up until then. But although the yacht's owner, Ian Cook of the Auckland superyacht

builder Yachting Developments, made a point of preserving as much of the boat's original structure as possible, when it came to the rig he chose to renew the aluminium mast and stainless steel rigging fitted in the 1960s instead of reverting to the original wooden spars. And, in order to take the strains of this high-stress rig, Cook had the hull sheathed in epoxy and fibreglass. As a result, when *Ranger* came to race in Europe two years later, although she performed well on the water, she was so heavily taxed by the new handicapping system in operation there that she was relegated to the bottom of her class – an unfortunate humiliation for one of New Zealand's most revered yachts.

Enthusiastic devotees

By then, authenticity had become the keyword in the classic yacht movement – particularly in Europe, where war was about to be declared on anyone who contravened the strict standards being established on the Mediterranean circuit. Yet, ironically, one of the best examples of the new ethos that was beginning to pervade was undertaken by a pair of newcomers who exemplified a new breed of "collector" owners now being attracted to the movement.

Frenchmen Robert Daral and Jean-Paul Guillet were, above all, collectors of antiques. For years the pair had bought and sold old cars and aeroplanes, and they had even speculated in those classic speedboats, the Italian-built Rivas. Neither of them had owned a sailboat, however, until Guillet stumbled across the derelict hull of an old wooden yacht on the quayside at St Malo. Typically, she had been converted to cruising with the addition of an ungainly cabin before being left high and dry to rot. Guillet fell in love with the shape of the hull, which reminded him of those stylish yachts he had noticed moored up on the quayside at St Tropez. Call it a collector's nose or beginner's luck, but his find turned out to be one of the last 12-Metres designed by William Fife III and built at Fairlie. A successful racer in her day, *Vanity V* was also one of the most exquisite boats that Fife ever drew.

Once Guillet and Daral realized the nature of their find, they spared no effort in having the yacht appropriately restored. Absolute beginners they might have been, but they were sensitive enough to treat an elderly lady in the style to which she had once been accustomed. Their first, crucial move was to bring together some key players to look after their charge. The Chantier de Guip in Brest, fresh from building the much-loved replica revenue cutter *La Recouvrance*, was put in charge of the rebuild work, while naval architect Guy Ribadeau Dumas – responsible for the restoration of the 1936 Nicholson cutter *Oiseau de Feu* and the 1906 Oertz 10-Metre *Pesa*, among others – was brought in to research the technical aspects of the project.

She was to be as original as possible, yet competitive on the Mediterranean circuit for which she was destined. The reasons for this were entirely pragmatic and in keeping with the owners' background

left One hundred years after first winning the cup named in her honour, the "pride of Melbourne" is sailing once more on Port Philip Bay. Designed by William Fife and built in Adelaide in 1897, *Sayonara* was completely rebuilt in 2000.

above *Sayonara* was fitted with a completely new rig, made to her original design. Much attention was paid to getting the period details right. Here, some neatly executed leathering on the running backstay helps prevent chafe.

as collectors rather than sailors. They hoped to sell the boat and make a profit, and the only way they could do that was to optimize the boat's value. "The yacht had to be restored as a collector's piece," said Guillet. "Compare it to a Spitfire, which sells for about the same price: it must be exactly as original, even if only 50kg of it actually is original, otherwise it doesn't have the same value."

The result was that everything, from the shape of the mouldings on the edges of the hatches to the position of the deck fittings, was researched and wherever possible returned to the original. Not a scrap of plywood was fitted onto *Vanity V*; even the decks – which nowadays are invariably laid over a plywood subdeck to keep the boat watertight – were replaced with solid timber. The steel floors, usually welded together, were riveted by the Arsenal at the nearby naval dockyard, and the deck fittings were all reproduced either directly from the originals or from contemporary castings. And, although the galley was moved aft from its original position forward of the mast to allow more stowage space for sails, Dumas was at pains to point out that a mattress could be laid over it to replicate the old quarter berth if required. On the other hand, the cedar timber Fife is thought to have used to build the accommodation was considered too cheap compared to the rest of the restoration and mahogany was used instead.

When *Vanity V* took to the water again in Brest in August 2000, she was one of the most authentic 12-Metres on the circuit and, either by luck or instinct, her owners had caught the spirit of a new era that was just beginning to dawn. It was the culmination of an increasingly purist movement which had started with *Altair* and now found expression again in *Vanity V*. Increasingly, the standards set by her restoration would become accepted as the norm.

above left Better known for his Vendée Globe-winning modern racing yachts, French designer Guy Ribadeau Dumas has applied his expertise to several important restoration projects, including the elegant Fife 12-Metre *Vanity V*.

above Although *Vanity V* was fitted with winches when she was launched in 1936, additional ones have been fitted and existing ones have been beefed up to cope with the large genoa she now carries to be competitive.

right Ribadeau Dumas's attention to detail means that *Vanity V* is now one of the most authentic 12-Metres afloat. There's not a scrap of plywood on her and even the steel floors were riveted rather than welded to replicate the original.

Setting the Standards

By the end of the 20th century, the classic yacht movement was in full swing. An apparently inexhaustible supply of newly restored classics joined the circuit every year, and more and more events were laid on for them. From being the passion of a few eccentric individuals, owning a classic had become fashionable and, as such, was becoming increasingly absorbed into yachting's mainstream. The active participation of celebrities such as the Gucci family and actor Jeremy Irons gave the sport added glamour and helped to dispel its rugged sou'wester and Stockholm tar image. The fact that cutting edge America's Cup yacht designers such as Doug Peterson, Germán Frers and Ed Dubois owned and raced classic yachts suggested that these old boats were still exciting to race.

left The detailed research and meticulous workmanship that went into the restoration of *Partridge* paid off when she started racing on the Prada circuit. A favourable rating, combined of course with some natty sailing, ensured she collected bucketloads of silver.

In the broader context, the end of the millennium focused people's minds not only on what the human race might aspire to, but also on what it had already achieved. And in the world of yachting, the achievements of the past were clearly visible in the elegant designs and dependable construction of older boats.

Haphazard handicaps

But as the numbers of yachts and events grew, so the mismatch between the different types of boats became more apparent. It had long been recognized that there would never be enough identical entries in most classes to allow level racing, therefore the clubs organizing the regattas had adopted a variety of handicapping rules to enable these wildly different types of craft to race together. The problem with handicapping – which is common to all mixed yacht racing – was exacerbated for classic yachts by the fact that these boats were all being restored by different yards, in different countries, and to different standards. While one yard might consider it acceptable to use modern boatbuilding techniques and materials, and merely preserve the appearance of the original, another might be at pains to replicate every detail of the original design and construction. The outcome would be two very different boats with very different racing characteristics, yet they might race in the same class and be given the same handicap.

Added to that, each club had its own idea of how boats should be handicapped, which meant competitors would get a different rating

above The French walnut interior of the Fife 15-Metre *The Lady Anne* evokes the style of 1912, when she was built. Under the CIM ratings system, however, she is penalized for having a microwave in her galley and teak instead of pine decks.

right But it was *The Lady Anne*'s mast that really got them going. Although built of wood by none other than Cowes sparmaker Harry Spencer, the inside was lined with carbon fibre. This was an anathema to CIM, which eventually banned her from racing.

next page *The Lady Anne*'s main rival was the only other gaff-rigged 15-Metre, the sublime *Tuiga*. Although considerably slower on the water, *Tuiga* invariably beat her Fife sister on paper thanks to her more favourable rating.

for every race they entered: at one event two boats might tie in the corrected results, at another they might finish well apart. Simply put, the problem was that there were no universal standards either for restorations or for race handicapping. The issue was particularly acute in the Mediterranean, where increasingly large numbers of classic restorations were being concentrated.

The solution was as daring as it was controversial. Under the aegis of the Comité International de la Méditerranée (CIM) – an organization created in 1926 to oversee races in the Mediterranean but which had become moribund – a group of classic boat aficionados devised a set of rules that they proposed to apply to all the regattas being held in France, Italy, and Spain. The new rules were effectively an amalgam of those used by the Nioulargue organizers and those operated by the Italian classic boat federation, Associazione Italiana Vele d'Epoca (AIVE). Broadly speaking, the rules divided the fleet into three age groups: Vintage (pre-1950), Classic (1950–75), and Spirit of Tradition (1976 onwards). Within these groups the boats were subdivided by rig (gaff or bermudan) and, if there were enough boats to warrant it, by size (usually under or over 66ft [20m]) – the minimum size limit was set at 25ft (7.6m).

In an attempt to level the playing field still further, the rules also contained a system of handicapping each boat. Like all rating rules, the starting point for the CIM system is a long formula composed mainly of such prosaic measurements as the boat's length, beam, and sail area. The resulting rating, inserted into another formula, gives an Allowance Per Mile (APM), and this is the amount of time subtracted from the boat's real (or elapsed) time for every mile it sails. At the end of the race, the APM is taken off the elapsed time and a corrected time is produced. While most of the latter-day rules had given boats a rating based simply on their physical dimensions, the new rules also rated them according to their degree of authenticity; in effect, the more original the boat, the better its rating, and vice versa.

Unlike most handicapping rules the CIM system has coefficients in its formula, which rate the boats on factors such as keel shape, rig, and age. For example, a boat with a long keel and big overhangs is taxed more heavily than one with a shallow keel and plumb (upright) ends; a gaff-rigged schooner will fare better than a bermudan sloop; an old boat will win a more favourable rating than a young one. But it is the "authenticity and conformity" coefficient that has had the greatest impact and caused the most controversy. Under this rule, any changes from the vessel's original construction, rig, deck layout, and accommodation are penalized. Fit a plywood deck, you're penalized; add a few extra winches, you're penalized; use a self-furling jib, you're penalized. And the rules apply below decks as much as above: altering the accommodation or even fitting modern conveniences such as an electric toilet or microwave oven are also penalized.

An influential system

More than just a yacht racing rule, the CIM system was designed to evaluate and ultimately to influence the way in which boats were being restored. For, once owners knew their boat would attract a better rating by being restored as closely as possible to the original, they were likely to ask their friendly boatbuilder to take this into consideration because, after all, no matter how perfect the varnishwork, ultimately every owner likes to see their boat win. Thus, the CIM rule had the potential to profoundly affect the shape of our maritime heritage. It was, more than most such systems, evangelical.

And that, according to Bernard d'Alessandri, president of the Classic Yacht Division of CIM, was no accident. He freely admits that the CIM rule was about a lot more than just racing. "Competition is only a pretext to use the boat – it's not the ultimate goal," said d'Alessandri. "The most important thing is the maintenance of the fleet and the preservation of a culture. For that, we need owners, and the best way of keeping owners interested is by having regattas. They are a tool to provide spectacle and to help us know better the soul of a boat. But you must remember, many of these boats were not built to race. If you want competitive racing, you should buy another type of boat. The important thing is to keep the spirit of the craft alive so we can leave a beautiful thing behind for our children."

A new development in 1999 made the need for a universal standard in the Mediterranean even more urgent. For years there had been talk of grouping the various regattas into an official race series, and the fledgling International Classic Yacht Association (ICYA), based in the UK under the leadership of Tim "Spike" Killingback, and Fife expert and skipper Iain MacAllister, had already created its own grand prix by collating the results of the main events around Europe. This initiative was, however, quickly eclipsed when the clubs organizing the various Mediterranean regattas joined forces to create their own series – and, unlike the ICYA, they had the financial clout to see it through, having secured headline sponsorship from Italian fashion house Prada.

The first Prada Challenge for Classic Yachts was launched in 1999, starting with the Prada Veteran Boat Rally at Porto Cervo in Sardinia and moving on to Monaco, Cannes, and St-Tropez. The following year events in Spain and mainland Italy were added to the series. From the outset, the Prada Challenge was organized in conjunction with the CIM and used its racing rules – including the controversial handicapping system – to regulate all its races. The Prada Challenge headquarters was the Yacht Club de Monaco, whose director general was none other than d'Alessandri.

The Prada series consolidated what had already become a well established circuit of regattas, with feeder races linking one event to the next. The smart red Prada flash endorsed and gave added caché to a scene already obsessed with image (the CIM rules contained a clause that could penalize and ultimately ban any boat that wasn't being kept up to scratch). But while the glittering armada continued to line up on the quayside, resplendent in its acres of glowing varnish and shining brasswork and revelling in its newfound Prada glory, back in the shoreside bars it was the CIM ratings that everyone was talking about.

The first casualty

One of the first boats to be hit by the new rules was the newly-restored *The Lady Anne*. Ever since the Fife 15-Metre *Tuiga* had burst onto the scene in 1993, she had wowed spectators and competitors alike with her low sheer and vast clouds of sail. There was nothing quite like her, and the Yacht Club de Monaco soon snapped her up as their flagship. Then in 1999 *The Lady Anne*, another Fife 15-Metre, was relaunched after an extensive rebuild by Fairlie Restorations, and it seemed as if *Tuiga* would at last have a sister to play with. Although arguably not quite as pretty as her predecessor, *The Lady Anne* had an even greater sail area and was a welcome new addition to the circuit. The trouble was, she didn't conform to the CIM rules. Because the owner planned to sail the yacht widely all over Europe, as a safety precaution some of the spars had been lined with carbon fibre to prevent them breaking and causing damage to boat and, more importantly, crew. This was clearly in breach of the CIM rules, which state that spars must be either wood or aluminium. On that count, and on a number of other features, including the ubiquitous microwave, *The Lady Anne* was heavily penalized and given a rating of –39 compared to *Tuiga*'s +73. In effect this meant she gave her sister ship three minutes for every mile raced, making it virtually impossible

pages 136–7 Evening in St Tropez during the celebrated La Nioulargue Regatta. A vastly disparate fleet race together, and park together, under the "classics" banner. Some sort of rating system is required to create a more level playing field.

previous page Two crew perch on the masts of the Herreshoff schooner *Mariette* to ensure the topsails are set on the right side of the gaffs. Even with modern winches and lighter sails, you still need a large crew to operate a traditional rig.

right The 1935 Arch Logan cutter *Tawera* chases the competition during the Logan Classic Yacht Regatta in Auckland. The event was staged to coincide with the last two America's Cup series in 2000 and 2003 and shone a spotlight on the revival of classics in New Zealand.

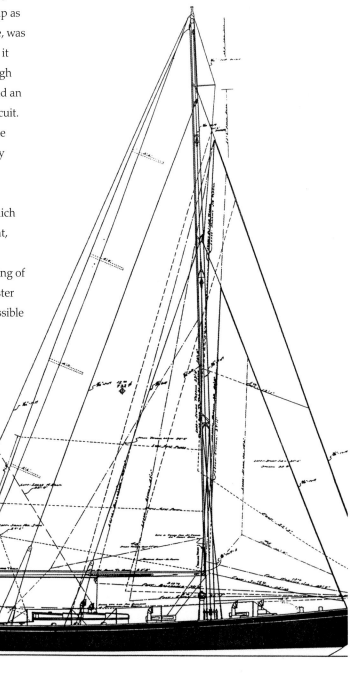

right Wherever possible, original line drawings are used to ensure yachts are restored as authentically as possible. Even minor deviations from the original design can affect the vessel's rating and may make her uncompetitive on the race circuit. This is the sail plan of *Stormy Weather*.

– even though she was invariably several miles ahead on the water – for her to beat *Tuiga* on handicap.

The Lady Anne's Australian skipper Paul Goss felt understandably aggrieved. "Carbon fibre makes up only 15 per cent of the spars and is there purely to add strength rather than give stiffness or save weight. It gives us minimal advantage compared to having winches, especially going around the buoys," said Goss. "We're here to enjoy the regatta, but we don't want to be handicapped out of it."

Yet that is exactly what happened. On top of her huge handicap, the CIM organizers gave *The Lady Anne* two years to "clean up her act" and get herself some new, carbon fibre-free spars, or else face being banned from racing. And, because by the late '90s CIM controlled all the main events on the Mediterranean circuit, their threat carried considerable weight. Sadly, the yacht's owner refused to comply deciding instead to sail his beautiful yacht in alternative waters, including several northern European regattas. It was a great loss to the Mediterranean racing scene in general and to the burgeoning 15-Metre revival in particular, but d'Alessandri, who usually helms *Tuiga* on behalf of the Yacht Club de Monaco, was unrepentant: "Where do you draw the line? If you allow carbon fibre this year, you might get uranium or titanium keels next year," he said. "In 150–200 years there will be very few old boats left. If we let people massacre a boat and then just keep the name, there won't be any left at all."

As in all handicapping systems, there were winners as well as losers. The 1885 cutter *Partridge*, meticulously restored as closely as

previous page Over in the UK, the big event of 1998 was the first Fife Regatta on the Clyde, organized to "race and celebrate William Fife". It was such a success it was repeated in 2003, when the 1923 ketch *Kentra* displayed her Fife magic.

above Authenticity was key in restoring the 1933 Anker & Jensen 12-Metre *Vema III* at Walsteds in Denmark. Although it would have been cheaper to build a new interior, co-owner Tor Jørgen Dahl insisted the original was preserved wherever possible.

right *Vema III* was queen of the ball at the Europe Week regatta on the Oslofjord in 2000, when 120 yachts gathered for two weeks of sailing under the auspices of the European Classic Yacht Union. The event was billed as "a cultural voyage to yesteryear".

possible to original (see p130), received a phenomenal +188 APM and scooped up the silver wherever she went. For co-owner and skipper Alex Laird it was just rewards for 18 years of hard toil and, predictably, he gave the rating his thumbs-up: "No system is completely foolproof, and it will be different in different weather with different boats, but generally it tends to work," said Laird. "Being a purist, I'm in favour of the emphasis on originality if it encourages new boats to be more original. It's not all just about racing."

A fitting tribute

While everyone on the Med circuit was getting hot under the collar about their ratings, traditionalists up north were too busy partying to worry about such esoteric matters. The 100th birthday of Eric Tabarly's Fife cutter *Pen Duick* was the excuse for a fine knees-up at his home town of Bénodet in Brittany in May 1998. A select collection of Fifes gathered for three days of sailing and celebration in honour of the yacht that more than any other could lay claim to being France's flagship. Just two weeks later, while sailing *Pen Duick* to Scotland, France's most famous sailor fell over the side 35 miles (65km) south-west of Milford Haven. His body was recovered a few weeks later.

Tabarly's death cast a shadow over the event he and his beloved yacht had been about to join: the first Fife Regatta. Maritime artist and Fife enthusiast Alastair Houston, along with his sister Fiona, had organized what promised to be one of the most exclusive classic yacht regattas ever: a gathering of boats built by William Fife III starting and finishing less than a mile from where they were originally launched, at his yard in Fairlie. Although little now remains of the yard, a couple of the village streets carry its name and the church spire is topped by a gilded model of the yawl *Latifa*, launched at the yard in 1936.

Some 11 boats turned up for that first event, ranging from the 98ft (30m) ketch *Kentra* to the 25ft (7.6m) Conway & Menai Strait One-Design *Starlight*, most of them returning for the first time since they were launched. The week-long regatta took the fleet racing on the Clyde and adjacent waters where so many Fifes once had sport before the war. The regatta received wide acclaim and, despite swearing never to do it again, the Houston siblings were persuaded to organize a second one in June 2003, which this time played host to twice the number of competitors.

Up north and Down Under

In Scandinavia the newly-formed European Classic Yacht Union (ECYU) launched a new series of Europe Weeks, inspired by the regattas of the same name held at various locations around Europe before World War I. Like the Fife Regattas, the ECYU events were ambitious affairs, made up of a mixture of around-the-buoys races and longer passage races, spread over one and sometimes two weeks,

left The distinctive William Fife dragon emblazoned on her spinnaker leaves no doubt who *Flica II* was designed by. With her semi-professional crew, the German-owned 12-Metre did well during racing at the 2000 Europe Week in Norway.

above Founder of the Europe Classic Yacht Union, Peter Ennals restored his first boat when he was 12 and later helped set up a wooden boatbuilding school outside Oslo. He was also instrumental in organising the popular Europe Week series.

and usually including visits to significant local yachting landmarks. Staged annually since 1998, the first was held in and around Stockholm; the next by the River Blackwater, Essex in the UK; then the Oslofjord, Norway in 2000, Latvia in 2001; Lac Leman, Switzerland in 2002; and Denmark in 2003.

With the Kiwis' first defence of the America's cup in Auckland in 2000, the New Zealand Classic Yacht Association (NZCYA) used the lull between the Louis Vuitton series – which determines the Cup's challenger – and the America's Cup to stage a week-long regatta of its own – the Logan Classic Yacht Regatta (named for its clothing company sponsor rather than the boatbuilder). It was an inspired piece of timing, plugging into the festive spirit of the America's Cup and guaranteeing the largest, most international, and most boat-oriented audience ever likely to be gathered in Auckland. There was even a handful of visiting classic yachts sailed over specifically for their owners to watch the Cup – most notably, *Velsheda*, *Belle Aventure*, and *Mariella* – which happily switched from spectators to performers for the week.

But the undisputed heroes of the Logan Classic Yacht Regatta was the fleet of 30ft to 40ft (9–12m) local A-class yachts, with their dramatically low sheers and fine lines. It was a credit to the efforts of the NZCYA, and the revival of interest in classic yachts in New Zealand that it has spawned, that so many fine examples of these yachts were racing once again. Many of them had been restored to their original rigs and, although most weren't finished to quite the same uncompromising standards as their Mediterranean counterparts, there was no denying the grace of their lines or their speed on the water.

Although light winds put a bit of a damper on the racing, the Logan Classic Yacht Regatta was repeated during the next America's Cup in 2003, when New Zealand lost the cup to the Swiss challenger, *Alinghi*. With the next America's Cup in 2007 being defended by the Swiss at Valencia in Spain, the heyday of the regatta may already be over, but it has served its purpose by showcasing New Zealand's unique fleet of classic yachts. That, combined with the visit to Europe of two of the top Kiwi classics, *Ranger* and *Thelma*, has raised the profile of the country's maritime heritage far higher than can have seemed possible only 10 years ago.

A grand jubilee

But the event that classic-boat enthusiasts the world over were most excited about was the America's Cup Jubilee at Cowes in 2001, organized to celebrate the 150th anniversary of the 1851 race around the Isle of Wight, which eventually formed the basis of the America's Cup. It was billed as "the greatest yachting regatta ever" which wasn't entirely hyperbole.

above After years languishing in Townsville, Australia, the 23-Metre *Cambria* was restored in 1995. Many of her original bronze fittings were found stored in her bilges. A neat dial on the steering wheel mechanism indicates what position the helm is in.

right *Cambria* was shipped up from Australia and restored to her original cutter rig specially for the America's Cup Jubilee in 2001. At 114ft (34.2m) long, she is thought to be the largest yacht designed by William Fife III still in existence.

More than 200 invited yachts from around the world, most of them classics, gathered together to take part in eight days of racing and partying. Many of the great names in the classic yacht world were there, including *Ticonderoga, Bloodhound, Stormy Weather, Dorade, Tuiga, Hallowe'en, Belle Aventure, Germania VI,* and *Mariette* – plus all three surviving J-Class yachts. The 1928 Fife 23-Metre *Cambria* was shipped up from Australia and rerigged specially for the occasion, from New Zealand there was Auckland's "working class hero" *Ranger* along with her modern counterpart, the 1992 America's Cup trial series winner NZL-32, otherwise known as *Black Magic*. The New York Yacht Club arranged to have 32 yachts transported across the Atlantic by container ship. Significantly, all were racing under CIM rules – the largest event to have been put under their jurisdiction to date.

Perhaps most awesome though was the magnificent collection of 12-Metre yachts tied up in the main yacht basin every evening, some 37 of them, including four former America's Cup winners. This was the largest ever gathering of 12-Metres and their names came straight out of the history books: *Trivia, Northern Light, Flica II, Nyala,* and the America's Cup winners *Columbia* and *Intrepid*. Even the infamous *Australia II*, sailed for the first time since 1983 by her America's Cup-winning crew, was allowed out of her usual home at the Western Australian Maritime Museum to join her classmates. She must have been the only boat there whose every part has been itemized and catalogued for posterity.

Several yachts were dismasted and some crew were injured in the heavy winds that marked the first day's racing, but the weather soon cleared and gave way to a week of almost Mediterranean-like conditions. The event culminated with a race around the island, just one day shy of exactly 150 years since America's epoch-making victory. Ashore, guests at the myriad social events included the Aga Khan and Sir Richard Branson alongside luminaries of the yachting world, from designer Olin Stephens to America's Cup skippers Dennis Conner and Russell Coutts. The regatta offered a unique opportunity to see so many of the people and boats at the heart of the sport all gathered in one place.

As well as being a memorable event in its own right, the America's Cup Jubilee was the catalyst for several restoration projects which, once they had signed up for the event, used it as the deadline for completion. At least one, the 12-Metre *Onawa* co-owned by Elizabeth Meyer, was rebuilt specifically for the event. Among the most notable newcomers was the 1916 *Marilee*. One of only four surviving New York 40s, she was restored by the Cannell Boatbuilding Co in Camden, Maine, for a syndicate of New York owners. Launched only a few weeks before the Jubilee, *Marilee* broke her boom on the first day but carried on and sailed the rest of the week with a roughed-out replacement by Cowes rigger Harry Spencer. She finished the regatta

left The elegant *Solway Maid* was the last yacht to be built by William Fife III. Launched in 1939, she has survived in largely original condition, but lost the top of her mast when she was dismasted on the first day of the America's Cup Jubilee.

above Shinning in the rigging. A crew on *The Lady Anne* slides back down to deck level after untangling a halyard. All crew are issued with the obligatory white cotton "Popeye" uniforms before going sailing, and deck shoes are optional.

next page The high point of the 2001 America's Cup Jubilee was the race around the Isle of Wight, recreating the famous race 150 years before. After rounding the Needles, the Herreshoff schooner *Mariette* sets a cloud of sail heading for the finish line.

in second place in her class, right behind Halsey – descendant of Nat
– Herreshoff and his *Rugosa*.

Marilee went on to be very active on the classic boat circuit on
both sides of the Atlantic and, although intended as something of a
flagship for the New York Yacht Club, she was sold in 2003 for a
rumoured $1 million. Such a sum may seem an extortionate price to
pay for a 40ft (12m) yacht well past its prime, but it was symptomatic
of a new attitude towards these old boats. Federico Nardi's concept of
the "floating painting" was catching on with an audience outside Italy,
and people were starting to talk about classic yachts as collectible
"artifacts". With such heightened awareness, the value of these yachts
grew accordingly, and suddenly those at the top end – particularly
those by well-known designers, such as a Fife, Herreshoff or Logan –
began to look like marketable propositions. The astronomical cost of
restoration and maintenance were now outweighed by the price some
newly-restored yachts were fetching.

By definition, however, there was a finite number of old yachts left
in the world to be restored, particularly of good pedigree. The solution,
of course, was to build new yachts to the old designs and thus enjoy all
the advantages of an old boat without the worry of an ageing structure.
Yet considering the extremely high cost of rebuilding elderly wooden
craft, classic boat aficionados were remarkably slow to take up this
option, particularly in Europe. For collectors and sailors alike it appears,
nothing compared to the kudos of owning the genuine article.

Restoration versus new-build

Yet the ethical argument for building new boats rather than restoring
old ones is compelling. If future generations are to learn about yacht
building techniques of the 1930s, it's clearly more instructive to study
the remains of a yacht built in that period rather than a project from
the 1990s, complete with all the compromises that are an inevitable
part of any rebuild. Indeed, many old boats are so extensively rebuilt
during their so-called restorations that little, if anything, is left of the
original – in the case of the 15-Metre *The Lady Anne* the only original
items remaining are the two mainsheet bollards. *Velsheda* is virtually
new, and of the original *Endeavour* only parts of her sternpost and
items of gear are original. And *Pen Duick*'s hull is of glass fibre, the old
wooden hull having been past repair. For this reason alone, there is a
strong case for building a replica of an historic yacht and preserving
the original (albeit crumbling) structure in a museum.

Set against this is the argument that, by the time the boats have
reached this stage they have usually been so extensively converted,
repaired, and generally mucked about with that there is little of the
old boat left anyway.

Whether to conserve in a museum or return an historic vessel to
the water came to a head over the fate of sailing novel *The Riddle of the*

left The 49ft (14.7m)
Rhodes yawl *Carina*
awaits restoration outside
the International Yacht
Restoration School in
Newport, Rhode Island,
USA. When her time
comes, her restorers
will face the ongoing
dilemma of deciding how
much should be restored
and how much should
be rebuilt.

above A line of Beetle
Cats is rebuilt by students
at the International Yacht
Restoration School. Many
of the boats will have to
be completely reribbed
and largely replanked as
part of the training
programme. But are they
then new or old boats?
That's the old chestnut.

Sands author Erskine Childers' old boat *Asgard*. The 50ft (15m) Colin Archer-designed yawl had acquired something of a mythical status having been used by Childers for gun-running to Irish Republicans prior to his execution in 1922. Converted for sail training in the 1960s and '70s, she lay derelict for several years before eventually being put under cover and exhibited in Kilmainham goal in Dublin.

In the late 1990s, the Asgard Restoration Group – which included the Irish government minister whose department owns *Asgard*, as well as the current head of the Childers family – was formed with the intention of restoring the yacht to sailing condition. The problem was that, in order to make her seaworthy, much of the original structure, some 90 per cent of which was thought to be original, would probably have to be replaced. Incensed by the thought of losing the very decks that Childers himself must have paced, an opposition lobby was established to try to preserve the vessel as a museum artefact. One of the members of that group was another Irish government minister, the head of Arts and Heritage, whose department would have to give permission before *Asgard* could be released for restoration. Latest news seemed to suggest that the conservationists were likely to lose this particular battle.

Another so-called restoration that caused a furore in the mid-1990s was that of the 150ft (46m) schooner *Adela* (ex-*Heartsease*). When the 1903-vintage yacht was taken to the Pendennis Shipyard in Falmouth in 1994, it was widely assumed that a traditional restoration was about to take place. As the interior was stripped out and the hatches cut off and piled up on the quayside, it seemed that a major rebuild was on the cards. When the chainsaws started to cut up the hull into bonfire-sized chunks, however, suspicions were finally raised.

After much outcry, the yard eventually admitted that a survey had shown that the hull was beyond restoration and that a new hull was being built which would incorporate as many of the old features as possible. It turned out that the new hull was being built of steel, as opposed to the original wood, and since not much of the old joinery was compatible with the new design most of that was jettisoned too. The relaunched vessel was to all intents and purposes a new boat, albeit bearing the name of a once-famous yacht.

Although these events caused an outcry among classic-boat enthusiasts, they were powerless to do anything about it and an irreplaceable piece of maritime heritage was lost forever. But although the preservationists had lost another battle, the case served as a sharp warning of the dangers of historic old boats falling into the wrong hands and, ultimately, the furor it created strengthened the case for preservation. Significantly, *Adela* was allowed to join the Mediterranean classic yacht circuit, but she was placed firmly in the Spirit of Tradition class, destined to racing with other" modern classics".

above One of the stars of the Fife Regatta in 2003 was the 1914 cutter *Moonbeam IV* – newly-restored in Burma and sailed back to Europe in time for the gathering on the Clyde. The winner of the 1920 King's Cup didn't win any races this time however.

right Sunrise off Rothesay in Scotland. The 1904 *Mikado* takes a rest in between thrashing her much larger rivals during the 2003 Fife Regatta. For everyone there, the event was as much about scenery and culture as it was about racing.

Instant
Classics

The unexpected strength of the classic yacht revival once it did get under way had some surprising consequences. Whereas a couple of decades before there seemed to be a glut of old boats looking for malleable owners to save them, by the turn of the millennium it looked as if there might not be enough vintage craft to go around. The solution was of course to build new classics. The degree to which modern materials and modern design concepts were incorporated into these new-builds, however, would be the subject of much heated debate.

left The Fife-designed *Seabird* is everyone's idea of what a small classic yacht should look like. Yet her hull was built in cedar strip and sheathed with epoxy, and her cream-coloured sails are 100 per cent synthetic. Her design is over 100 years old.

Despite the snob value attached to owning a genuine vintage classic, as the number of old boats left to be restored diminished, replica-building became an increasingly logical option. Perhaps because of the relative shortage of restoration projects in the country, the United States had a long tradition of building new boats to old designs – although still on a minuscule scale compared to the number of fibreglass boats being churned out by the mainstream yards.

Although a few well-established yards such as Gannon & Benjamin at Martha's Vineyard prided themselves on building only wooden boats, another US yard was set up uniquely on the principal of building replicas of famous designs - and those by L Francis Herreshoff in particular. Legendary Yachts at Washougal, Washington started in 1994 by building a replica of Herreshoff's favourite and most famous design, the ketch *Ticonderoga*. But although the yard was faithful to the original lines, the 72ft (22m) hull was built of composite wood/steel, the mast was made of carbon fibre, and the interior was upgraded to incorporate modern-day "essentials" including a generator, a washing machine, and a watermaker. *Radiance*, as she was named, proved an impressive calling card for the newly-formed company and was followed by a string of other Herreshoff designs, including the 33ft (10m) *Araminta* and the 57ft 6in (17.5m) *Bounty*, which won the *Cruising World* magazine Boat of the Year award in 2002.

In Europe, the trend towards replica-building was more gradual, and once again it was France which led the way. Some 10 years after the success of the Bateaux des Côtes scheme to replenish the country's stock of traditional working boats, in the late 1990s the French turned their attention to yachts. Two of the first were a couple of replicas of boats by the Impressionist artist-turned-yacht-designer, Gustave Caillebotte (1848–94). Two of his most successful designs were 30-Square-Metre yachts *Roastbeef* and *Lézard*. As the centenary of Caillebotte's death approached, a Paris-based group decided to build a replica of *Roastbeef*. They were soon followed by another group in Marseille who opted to build a replica of *Roastbeef*'s rival, *Lézard*, in order to match race with the Parisian boat and settle the long-running debate about which was the fastest.

Like the craft in the Bateaux des Côtes scheme, both Caillebotte boats were built as near-replicas, with traditional plank-on-frame hulls and solid timber decks. *Roastbeef* was launched into the Seine in 1996, while the new *Lézard* slipped into the warmer waters of the Mediterranean in 1997. When the pair eventually competed later that year the results were inconclusive, with each boat winning a race. Perhaps their respective crews decided it was best not to dash the century-old mystic of these two legendary yachts with the earthly reality of race results.

The first replicas

previous page After restoring a string of classic yachts, Ed Kastelein decided to build a new one, inspired by the lines of the Grand Banks schooners. The 140ft (42m) *Zaca a te Moana* was launched in 1992 and was part of a new vogue for building "modern classics".

left A nimble crew attempts to disentangle *Eleonora*'s topsail during racing at the Antigua Classics. The Dutch yacht is a near-replica of the famous *Westward* designed by Herreshoff in 1909 and considered the fastest schooner of her day.

above Most of the fittings on *Eleonora* are either straight replicas of the ones fitted on *Westward* or close adaptations. The yacht even has galvanized steel rigging, like *Westward*, which her owner claims is more reliable than stainless steel.

next page Old concept, new materials. The durability of wood/epoxy construction did away with many of the objections people had with "plank-on-frame" yachts, and paved the way to a new generation of wooden boats, such as the gaff cutter *Medusa*.

Beautiful as these Caillebotte boats were they had little basis in financial reality, having been built with funding from local government and charitable trusts. But a commercial build wasn't long in coming with what was, by all accounts, the first replica of a Fife design – and another first for France. Hubert Stagnol decided to build a small yacht to raise the profile of his yard at Bénodet in Brittany and, hopefully, win a few repeat orders. Having long admired Eric Tabarly's yacht *Pen Duick* sailing on the river nearby, it seemed natural enough to choose another William Fife design. With the Fife name inspiring almost unquestioning devotion among yachting folk, it made sense commercially too.

The boat Stagnol built was almost a miniature *Pen Duick*, with a clipper bow and counter stern - albeit compared to *Pen Duick*'s 49ft 6in (15m) *Seabird* was a mere 27ft 4in (8.3m) long overall and just 18ft 5in (5.6m) on the waterline. For simplicity of construction and for ease of maintenance, the hull was of modern strip plank and epoxy construction, with Oregon pine decks laid over a plywood subdeck. And, whereas the original 1889 version would doubtless have had galvanized steel fittings, the cost of building even a small wooden

boat in the 21st century means that the whole boat has to be "specced up" as much as possible in order to command the highest price - and that meant using bronze.

Seabird went on the market for around £56,000 in the summer of 2000 and orders for the mini-Fife soon started to come in; it wasn't exactly a flood, but it was enough for Stagnol to loft up a bigger sister, which was due for launching in 2004-5.

On a completely different scale, and this time built in Holland, was a near-replica of a famous American yacht, by a famous American designer. Nat Herreshoff's 136ft (41.4m) *Westward* was considered the fastest schooner of her day and in 1910, with skipper Charlie Barr at the helm, won 11 out of 11 races entered during her first season in Europe. Back in the US, she won the coveted Astor Cup the following year. After reading about her race history and seeing old photos of the yacht, Dutch restaurateur/entrepreneur Ed Kastelein became obsessed with the idea of building a new vessel to *Westward*'s lines. Kastelein had already undertaken a string of increasingly ambitious restorations, including *Aile Blanche*, *Thendara*, and *Ondine*, and had just sold his 121ft (37m) schooner *Zaca a te Moana*. He was ready for his biggest challenge yet.

Built by the Van der Graaf shipyard in Holland, the new yacht, *Eleonora*, was a faithful rendition of the Herreshoff lines, although a cut-out had to be made for the propeller and the hull construction was updated from riveted steel to welded steel plates. The rig was based on *Westward*'s cruising rig, which at 11,800sqft (1,096m²) is some 1,700sqft (158m²) smaller than her full racing rig. Likewise, most of the deck details were either copied straight from Herreshoff or developed from his original designs. Below decks, although the waterproof bulkheads required by modern safety regulations meant that the original *Westward* layout could not be adhered to, all of the joinery detailing was carefully researched and duplicated.

Kastelein was keen to convey that *Eleonora* was not simply a replica of *Westward*. "Replica is not the right word. If I buy a Rolex, it's not a replica of the original Rolex; it's just a Rolex," said Kastelein. "*Eleonora* was built to the same lines as *Westward*, but she's a different boat. That's why she has a different name. *Eleonora* is just *Eleonora*, a schooner built to a Herreshoff design and inspired by *Westward* and her near-sister ship *Elena*."

A logical anomaly

Eleonora was launched in 2000 and fully commissioned in 2002. With her vast expanse of empty deck space barely interrupted by the neat line of cabins running down the centre, and her enormous expanse of sail, she made a magnificent sight romping the course, first at the Antigua Classics and then on the Mediterranean circuit. But *Eleonora* presented race organizers with a dilemma: while as a modern replica

above Skipper David Burn steers a steady course on the "modern classic" *Whitefin* during racing at the prestigious La Nioulargue Regatta. The hexagonal binnacle and general "woodiness" are both trademarks of her designer Bruce King.

right Although built of wood, the 90ft (27m) Whitefin has an unashamedly modern rig, complete with hydraulic stay tensioners and electric winches. She set a trend for classically-styled, fast cruising yachts when she was launched in 1983. She powers along at over 11 knots.

next page Also designed by Bruce King but launched nearly 20 years after *Whitefin*, the 70ft (21.3m) *Misconduct* is quite a different beast. The acres of wood are still there, but the design is that of a comfortable cruiser/racer rather than a sleek racer/cruiser.

she should, strictly speaking, have been placed in the Spirit of Tradition class, she clearly had a lot more in common with the other long-keeled, gaff-rigged boats in the Vintage and Classic classes. Thankfully common sense prevailed, and most organizers put her in among the Classics.

That in turn created the anomaly of having a J-Class yacht *Velsheda* – built in the 1930s but rebuilt with modern amenities and high-powered, modern rigs – placed in the Spirit of Tradition class, while a brand new boat was placed with the Classics. But what may have seemed a contrary decision on paper made complete sense on the water: anyone judging the two yachts by appearances alone would assume that the glitzy J, with her rod rigging and banks of electric winches, was the newer boat and that the simply-rendered Herreshoff, with her minimal winches and galvanized rigging, was the grand old dame.

But *Westward* wasn't the only ghost from the old "Big Class" to be revived. For years there had been talk of building a replica of King George V's *Britannia*, arguably the most famous yacht of all time. It was a dream long espoused by a young, Isle of Wight-based, classic boat enthusiast – penniless but visionary – named Adam Appleton until his premature death in 1999. At the time it had seemed more fantasy than probability. What, then, would Appleton have made of the news that, within a few months of his death, the keels of not just one but two *Britannia* replicas were being laid? The first, led by a Norwegian 12-Metre enthusiast, was built at a yard in Archangel in Russia and was due to be commissioned in 2004, while the other, the 148ft (45m) *Harlequin*, was in-build in Holland.

And the Js were back. Incredible as it would have seemed only a decade or so before, yet 2003 saw the launch of the first new J-Class yacht to be built in more than 60 years. The replica of American designer Starling Burgess's 135ft (41m) *Ranger*, recognized the world over as "the ultimate J", was built by Danish Yachts at Skage in Denmark and was due to join her fellow Js for the 2004 season. Not long ago, the three remaining Js had appeared to be in terminal decline, but now, in the new millennium, not only were all three back on the water but also the class once consigned to history was being revived, and indeed growing.

Ersatz boats or modern classics?

Time for a recipe. Take the classic aesthetics of yesteryear, add the aerodynamics of a modern hull and a sprinkling of new hardware, mix it all up and bake it in epoxy and carbon fibre, and what do you have? An ersatz boat that doesn't know whether it's old or new, say some. A modern classic, say others. Aside from the odd layer of carbon fibre sneaked into a mast, or the occasional hull sheathed in epoxy, there is little that has divided the classic boat fraternity more than the advent

of the modern classic. To some aficionados the merest mention of "modern" and "classic" in the same sentence is likely to have them reaching for their caulking mallet to thump you over the head.

The history of the modern classic begins in 1976 when American designer Bruce King built a yacht called *Unicorn*. Although the 41ft (12.5m) ketch was an important milestone at the start of the wooden boat revival, she was a world apart from most of the other wooden boats being built at the time: *Unicorn*'s clipper bow and classic lines disguised a thoroughly modern construction employing the latest epoxy technology. Her success led King to design the 92ft (28m) *Whitehawk* with a similar concept, basing her lines on L Francis Herreshoff's masterpiece *Ticonderoga*. Although many bemoaned this doctoring of Herreshoff's work, the yacht also drew many admirers and proved fast on the water. Almost by stealth, the era of the modern classic had arrived.

The appeal of the type is obvious, however. If the design is right, you should end up with the look of a classic yacht combined with the performance and ease of handling of a modern boat, and without the heavy maintenance schedule of a genuine old classic.

Unicorn and *Whitehawk* were billed as modern interpretations of old designs, yet King's next major project went a step further. *Whitefin* was a completely new yacht in her own right and was, by virtue of her long ends and copious amounts of woodwork, regarded as a classic. In her method of construction, her modern underwater shape, and her advanced rig – complete with hydraulic backstay tensioners and electric winches – she was utterly modern. More than most designs of this era, the 1984 *Whitefin* struck a delicate balance between old and new. For she had many of the retro touches that would come to characterize King's designs and the modern classic yachts in general – the elliptical varnished counter and fancy deck joinery, for example – she also had a cleanness of line and a purposeful-looking rig that was unashamedly modern.

Period detail survives

King explains the thinking behind the type like this: "The line dividing traditional appearance and modern utility is blurred, and therefore requires each of our clients to choose exactly where it is to be drawn. Some of them would love to build a gaff-rigger with bright finished wooden masts, all bronze hardware, etc, but while they dream about it, their pragmatic side generally gains the upper hand, and they wind up with a modern rig, complete with furlers, hydraulic winches, and stainless steel deck hardware. This leaves the geometry of the hull topsides, deck structures, and interior joinery open for traditional treatment."

It was a theme the designers of this new breed of craft would return to time and time again, constantly shifting the emphasis

above Ease of handling is the name of the game on board the "modern classics". A neat stowage system on *Misconduct* ensures the anchor is easily secured without damaging the hull, while roller furling makes life easier for the crew.

right You wouldn't find this on an old classic: a classy stainless steel dual-speed electric winch fitted on *Misconduct*. The enormous advances in technology make "modern classics" easier to handle which in turn means they need less crew.

next page Bruce King's 140ft (42m) ketch *Hetairos* was one of the most admired boats on the circuit when she was launched in 1993. For many, she was the ultimate fantasy yacht, and announced the arrival of a new breed of classically styled superyachts.

between traditional and modern aesthetics. Sometimes their efforts were so self-consciously retro that they became kitsch; sometimes the basic design was so fundamentally modern that the classic detailing looked incongruous. But when the right balance was struck, the result was a brave new style in a class all of its own.

King's next two designs illustrated how the right balance could be struck whatever the parameters. They were also two of the most impressive yachts ever built and confirmed the growing trend towards ever-larger, ever-more spectacular superyachts.

At 125ft (38m) long, *Hetairos*, built at Abeking & Rasmussen in Germany, was an exercise in period detail. Her deck was positively bristling with shiny cowl vents, domed hatches, exquisite joinery, wooden tenders, and acres of gleaming varnish and stainless steel. The clipper bow, with its carved trailboard, and the arched windows on the main cabin positively screamed "classic yacht". Needless to say, all these elaborate classic motifs concealed a powerful, modern sailing machine with all the amenities of the most well-appointed luxury yacht. In anyone else's hands, *Hetairos* might have become gaudy and ostentatious, but King's eye for a sweet line somehow transformed it into an impressive spectacle.

Spanish-built *Alejandra*, on the other hand, with her endless sheerline, low freeboard, and wide, uncluttered decks, was more reminiscent of the original J-Class yachts. Like the Js, a simple cove line was the only decoration on her hull – not the easiest thing to achieve on an aluminium vessel – but unlike the Js she was fitted with a mini wing keel to keep her draught down. The 134ft (40.8m) yacht still ended up 12ft 7in (3.9m) deep, but that was about 3ft (0.9m) less that a similarly sized J. The period detailing was infinitely more restrained than that on Hetairos, yet Alejandra still had the irrefutable air of a classic. Below decks was a different story. King designed a fantastically arcane interior, complete with mahogany panelling, a fireplace, circular staircase, and intricate hand-carvings. This was full-on retro at its most opulent.

Hetairos and *Alejandra* caused a sensation. To the uninitiated, they looked like fantasy boats from an earlier era, and they would have been hard pressed to tell King's new yachts apart from the gleaming restorations moored nearby. Even the old die-hards – whatever they felt about these ostentatious displays of retro detail – had to admit that the boats looked good on the water. *Hetairos* and *Alejandra* proved that a modern designer could create a classic style which could be applied to any yacht, of any size. Suddenly it seemed as if there were no limits to what could be done.

King wasn't the only one designing modern classics. *Hetairos*'s predecessor, also called *Hetairos*, was a 70ft (21.3m) steel ketch built in Holland by Royal Huisman Shipyard in 1985. Although her lines were very similar to her German-built successor, the Dutch-built *Hetairos*

had much less period detailing and looked rather salty by comparison. Another offspring of Huisman's launched in 1994, the same year as *Alejandra*, was the 131ft (40m) schooner *Borkumriff III*. As well as her clipper bow, elliptical counter stern, and traditional cabin housing, *Borkumriff* sported a very traditional-looking gaff mainsail – albeit on a lightweight modern spar.

Smaller vessels

As the design language of the new breed grew clearer, a range of smaller designs began to appear. One of the most consistent contributors was Dutchman André Hoek. After spending years optimizing the sailing performance of the traditional Dutch lemsteraken yachts, in the mid-1980s Hoek turned his attention to the burgeoning modern classics trend. In yachts such as *Kim* he combined a traditional-looking cruising hull and superstructure above water, with a wing keel, elliptical spade rudder, recessed anodes, and folding propeller underwater. The success of his approach led to the creation of a new range of yachts called, rather pointedly Truly Classic series. At least a dozen yachts have been built to this concept, ranging from 56ft to 80ft (17–24m) in length. More than most, they exploit their classic credentials, with hull lines and conservative deckhouses reminiscent of early Sparkman & Stephens designs, and, of course, acres of woodwork on display. Once afloat, they look to all intents and purpose like a genuine classic, and only the high-tech rig is likely to give the game away.

A variation on the new/old theme was adopted by Steve White (son of Joel) and his crew at the Brooklin Boatyard in Maine. Instead of updating an old design, White decided to take a modern yacht and build it in wood. The yacht he chose was the Swede 55, designed in 1975 by Knud Reimers for construction

previous page Built in 1994, *Sapphire* was the first big modern classic from Dutch designer Andre Hoek, and the first to be built by the now-famous Holland Jachtbouw yard outside Amsterdam. The yacht's success launched a highly productive partnership.

left Crew stow sails on the bowsprit of *Adix*. Launched in Mallorca in 1984, the three-masted schooner was completely rebuilt six years later with a fin keel and a modern rig. At 213ft (64m), she is now one of the largest modern classics on the circuit.

right The success of the first *Truly Classic* design inspired a range of yachts by the same name. For the full new/old effect, try masking off the hull below the waterline with a piece of paper and then masking it off above the waterline.

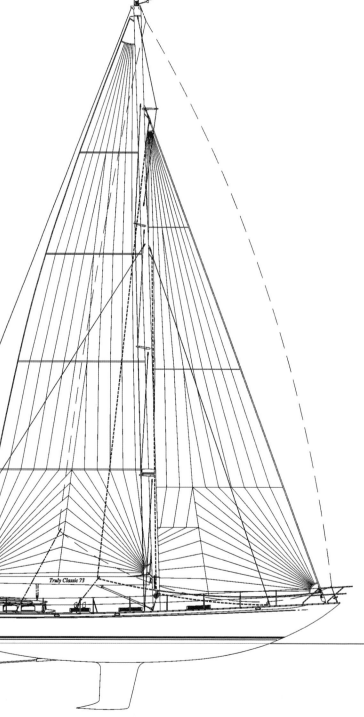

Truly Classic 73

in fibreglass. The result was an unquestionably fast boat which, after she was launched in 1990, had a habit of winning races wherever she went. The downside was that, until recently, *Vortex* didn't really fit into any of the existing racing classes – she was neither a modern boat nor a conventional classic – which led on more than one occasion to Steve disqualifying himself from accepting his silver. It would be nearly a decade before *Vortex* and other yachts like her were fully accepted on the classic yacht circuit.

Meanwhile, a strange transformation was taking place among some of the older classics. When she was originally built in Mallorca in 1984, *Adix* (ex-*Jessica*) was a fairly conventional, three-masted schooner, designed along similar lines to the 1930s schooner *Atlantic*. She was even fitted with two yards on her foremast to carry a pair of square sails on long downwind passages. Then, in 1990, she was sold to a new owner who decided to revamp the boat and transform her into a modern classic. Over a couple of years at the Pendennis Shipyard in Falmouth, England, under the management of skipper Paul Goss, the hull was lengthened from 203ft to 213ft (62–65m) and completely reshaped underwater – a contemporary fin keel replacing the traditional full-length keel. All the systems above and below decks were brought up to modern yacht standards, the rig updated for greater efficiency, and, of course, those troublesome squaresail yards were ditched.

When *Adix* emerged from the yard in 1991 she was almost unrecognizable; in just one year she had metamorphosed from classic to modern classic. And the transformation was as much to do with aesthetics as it was to do with any structural changes. The yard went on to perform a similar trick with the yacht *Adela* (ex-*Heartsease*) in 1995, but this time it was a 90-year-old vintage yacht they were turning into a modern classic and feelings among the classic boat fraternity turned to outrage (see p183).

The spirit of the modern classic

Elsewhere in England, a very different approach was being taken by a new company established by former McMillan Yachts boss Sean McMillan. Throughout the 1980s he had developed a reputation for building innovative, idiosyncratic wooden boats using the WEST System of epoxy/wood construction. In 1993 he teamed up with boatbuilder Mick Newman to build the first of what became a range of designs under the banner of Spirit Yachts. The first to be launched was a relatively modest 37-footer (11.3m) with a long counter stern, a fractional rig, and knocked-back masthead. An out-and-out racing yacht, she was fitted with a double cockpit and a small cuddy forward. But most extraordinary was her beam which, at just 7ft (2.1m), was reminiscent of those famous Scandinavian skerries racers.

left Ten years after they built their first yacht, a modest 37ft (11m) "pencil", Spirit Yachts took their new 70-footer *Ghost* to the South of France to play. The company chose their name several years before the Spirit of Tradition class was created.

above Drawn by Maine designer Robert Stephens, the 35ft (10.5m) *Tendress* combines many of the features of traditional yachts, such as the elegant overhangs and oval portholes, with modern conveniences, such as aluminium spars and roller-reefing genoa.

In fact, what McMillan and Newman had done was to take the attributes of a classic 30-Square-Metre, and given it a sophisticated, lightweight rig, and a modern underwater body complete with bulb keel and skeg rudder. With her black walnut trim and T-section boom, the Spirit 37 yacht looked liked nothing else afloat. Yet the concept caught the imaginations of a few more discriminating sailors – predictably mostly from Germany – and gradually the range expanded to include a 46- and 56-footer (14m and 17m). By 2003 the whole movement had grown sufficiently for McMillan and Newman to join the South of France circuit with their new 70-footer. Although a giant compared to her little sisters, who came along to celebrate the company's 10th birthday, she was moderate by comparison to many of the boats there.

"Ten years ago we were just whistling in the dark," Sean recalled, reflecting on the early days when the company was refused membership of the British Marine Industry Federation (the UK trade body) because it was not considered a serious proposition. "We didn't know if there really was a retro movement. We just built the boat we wanted that was fun and of a size that we could relate to. Luckily, it struck a chord. We're not interested in building pastiches of old yachts. We build out of wood because it's beautiful, but in design terms we are treading a delicate line between moving the boundaries on a bit and staying in the right aesthetic channel."

Across the pond, Donald Tofias was determinedly carving his own aesthetic channel. By the time he became active on the classic boat

above For a 76ft (22.8m) yacht, there's not a whole lot of space on *Wild Horses*, but then the boat was built primarily for racing rather than cruising. The standard of workmanship is the best you can get, however, courtesy of one of the top Maine boatbuilders.

right Low, beamy and with an easily-driven hull topped by a powerful modern rig, the W-46 is pretty to look at and exciting to sail. *Wild Horses* and her sister ship *White Wings* were intended to start a new class of classic racing yachts.

scene in the late 1990s, modern classics were a well-established phenomenon. For years he had owned a Starling Burgess cutter called *Arawak* (ex-*Christmas*), which – to the bemusement of many traditionalists – he had updated with a modern rig. But he wanted to go one better and build himself a boat that captured the grace and romance of the early 20th-century yachts – like the New York 30s and 40s designed by Nat Herreshoff – and yet had the performance of a modern racer. And he thought others might like to do the same thing, too. Tofias dreamed of nothing less than starting a whole new classic racing class, just like those NY30s and 40s of yesteryear.

It was an ambitious plan, but Tofias was an ambitious, and methodical, man. He chose as his designer one of the fathers of the wooden boat revival in the US, Joel White, while his builders would be two of the best-known yards in Maine: Rockport Marine and Brooklin Boatyard. The boat White came up with had a full 23ft (7m) of overhangs – nearly a third of the overall length – on a "canoe"-shaped hull with bulb keel and spade rudder. Fast, powerful, and beautiful to look at, it had relatively little accommodation for its length – but then it was intended primarily for racing.

To get the ball rolling, Tofias had two 76ft (23.1m) W-Class yachts built: *Wild Horses* was launched in the summer of 1998 and *White Wings* followed in the autumn of the same year. The two yachts made a striking sight racing together, first on the American and Caribbean circuits and then in the Mediterranean. But although the Ws had many fans, and the young crews that Tofias employed developed into something of a W family, at around $2 million apiece they didn't exactly fly off the shelf. Undeterred, Tofias had three smaller boats built to similar lines, which he christened the W-46s; one sold to someone in Maine, the other two joined the classic circuit on America's East Coast. So far, his dream of creating a new class with like-minded owners seems a long way off – but his persistence in promoting the cause of his boats and modern classics in general did much to rise awareness of the class.

A class of their own

While the popularity of modern classics among owners seemed to grow almost exponentially, getting the boats accepted at some of the established classic yacht regattas was proving more difficult. There remained a conviction among purists that the new boats would dilute the classics movement and that anything built of wood/epoxy, what some builders called "wood and schmoo", was, in any case, not a real wooden boat. Traditionalists resented modern designs which mimicked vintage craft then tried to muscle in on their events. A bit of clever design and some natty boatbuilding techniques were no substitute for generations of evolution and hard-won history.

The organizers of the Antigua Classics were among the first to recognize the problem. For years they had tolerated new boats in their Classics classes, until they finally came up with a solution in 1996, creating a whole new division which they called Spirit of Tradition. The idea caught on and before long there were Spirit of Tradition classes at most of the major regattas. Even the newly-formed CIM circuit, which had initially refused entry to Tofias and his W boats, eventually relented and incorporated a Spirit of Tradition class into their events. As ever, entry was strictly by invitation only, and so it remained at the organizers' discretion whether or not a boat was allowed to participate – a convenient final sanction that can exclude any yacht that for any reason is deemed unsuitable.

One of the most extreme of the new breed of yachts to challenge the traditionalists on a number of levels was a 90ft (27m) sloop called *Savannah*. With her uncluttered decks and graceful sheer – complete with 32ft (9.8m) of overhangs – she was little short of breathtaking. Her owner, Randolph Watkins, had studied the lines of two dozen yachts in order to work out the proportions that make up a perfectly-shaped hull. He concluded that the Fife cutter *Hallowe'en* and the

Nicholson J-Class yacht *Endeavour* came nearest to achieving his ideal. Designer David Pedrick was given the design brief and the Concordia boatyard in Massachusetts entrusted to build her.

Savannah was launched in April 1997 and her affinity to *Hallowe'en* was clear to see when the pair lay side by side at the Cannes Régates Royales a few years later. Below deck, the mahogany panelling gave off a rich glow and the deck beams overhead looked reassuringly solid. But hold on a moment. Why did those deck beams sound hollow when you knocked them? And why were there no frames lining the inside of the hull? You guessed. *Savannah* was built almost entirely of a carbon fibre/foam sandwich, including those deck beams with their beautifully moulded corners. Even parts of the interior joinery were made of wood veneers glued to a foam core as a weight-saving technique. Underwater she was fitted with a whale-tail fin keel, while above decks she boasted a high-aspect ratio bermudan rig and all the mechanical trappings of a modern yacht. Despite her impeccably classic aesthetics, *Savannah* was a thoroughly modern filly.

But all this trickery and doctoring of classic principles was as nothing compared to one small detail that Pedrick and Watkins had incorporated into their design. At the forward end of the cove line, recessed into the hull, they had "carved" a dragon's head. Now anyone who knows anything about classic boats knows that the dragon's head is William Fife's signature. No one else had ever had the audacity to copy his mark, and for some it was the final straw. It proved that these boats had no respect for the past.

Watkins disagreed: "These boats are a tribute to the great boats of the past. They aren't meant to compete against them but only to emulate their example and praise them," he said. "The dragon was only meant as a bit of fun and to demonstrate our genuine admiration of Fife."

Although "modern classics" remain an anathema to some sailors, they do represent the logical conclusion of a process that starts with an appreciation of the great classic yachts of the past. Given that ultimately there will not be enough of these boats in existence, it makes sense to build new ones out of wood. After that, it's a short step to using modern building techniques and sail technology, and an even shorter step to refining the hull shape to suit modern tastes.

What you end up with is a very different beast from a genuine classic, and the two should by no means be confused. Modern classics have evolved an original idiom of their own, however, which is no less deserving of a place in the magic circle of true vintage yachts. At the very least, they invite us to dream about what the Herreshoffs, and Fifes, and Nicholsons of this world would be building were they still around today. It might well be a yacht that would rightfully sail in the Spirit of Tradition.

left The future of classic yachting? Inspired by the great classics of the past, such as *Hallowe'en* and *Endeavour*, *Savannah* shows as sweet a line as any sailor could hope for. Yet her hull and all her major structural parts are made of carbon fibre.

above On deck, *Savannah* has a blend of old and new, the modern steering wheel and binnacle given a traditional twist with a touch of brass. Modern boatbuilding techniques mean that almost any combination of materials and styles is now possible.

Key events and restorations

1720   The first yacht club in the world, the Water Club of the Harbour of Cork, is founded.

1776   America's founding fathers sign the Declaration of Independence.

1800   William Fife I starts building boats on the beach at Fairlie on the Clyde.

1815   The Royal Yacht Squadron is founded in Cowes, UK.

1826   Yachting reaches new level of acceptability as the first Cowes Week Regatta is held on the Solent, UK.

1842   The USA's first yacht club, the Eastern Yacht Club of Boston, is founded.

1849   The Royal Van Lent Shipyard is founded on Kaag Island in Holland.

1851   Britannia rules the waves no more as the "low black schooner" *America* sails to Cowes and beats all comers.

1863   The Herreshoff boatyard is established in Bristol, Rhodes Island.

1870   Railroad entrepreneur James Ashbury makes Britain's first challenge for the America's Cup.

1878   Robert Logan sets up shop in Auckland, New Zealand.

1884   Benjamin Bénéteau sets up shop in Croix-de-Vie, France.

1886   William Fife III takes over the Fife yard at Fairlie.

1893   The King's yacht *Britannia*, designed by GL Watson, is launched.

1895–   Joshua Slocum sails around the world solo
1898   on *Spray*.

1900   Yachting is accepted as an Olympic sport.

1903   Herreshoff's Universal Rule is adopted in the USA, ultimately resulting in the creation of the J-Class 30 years later.

1905   Cpt Charley Barr crosses the Atlantic on the schooner *Atlantic* in 12 days – a record which remains unbroken for 75 years. The yard of Anker & Jensen is established in Norway.

1906   Ocean racing comes of age with the first New York (later Newport) to Bermuda race, followed by the first "Transpac" from California to Honolulu.

1907   Seemingly oblivious to the American Universal Rule, Europe creates its own International Rule, which results in yachts such as the 12-Metre class. The same year, the yard of Abeking & Rasmussen is established in Germany.

1925   The ex-Le Havre pilot cutter *Jolie Brise* wins the first Fastnet race, and later that year the Royal Ocean Racing Club is founded.

1926   The Fife cutter *Hallowe'en* sets a record in the Fastnet which remains unbeaten for 13 years.

1927   America accepts the International Rule for yachts rating 12-Metres and under.

1929   Sparkman & Stephens is founded. Their first major design *Dorade* is launched the following year and goes on to win the 1932 and 1933 Fastnet Races.

1930   The Americans trounce the Brits again as *Enterprise* beats *Shamrock V* 4:0 in the first America's Cup raced on J-Class yachts.

1936   The Royal yacht *Britannia* is scuttled off the Isle of Wight under the posthumous orders of King George V.

1942   Ray Greene of Toledo, Ohio builds the first fibreglass boat.

1944   William Fife III dies and his famous yard in Scotland is renamed Fairlie Yacht Slip under Archibald McMillan.

1945   It's the end of another legend as the Herreshoff Manufacturing Co shuts up shop. Meanwhile, John Illingworth wins the first Sydney to Hobart Race.

1952   Eric Tabarly rebuilds the hull of his 1898 Fife cutter *Pen Duick* in fibreglass.

1957   Coleman Boat & Plastics Co in California build *Bounty II*, the first production fibreglass cruising yacht.

1958   The America's Cup switches to the more affordable 12-Metres class.

1963   In the UK a bunch of not-so-old gaffers set up the Old Gaffers Association.

1964   Bénéteau builds its first range of fibreglass boats, the *Rétan* and the *Guppy*.

1965 Twenty boats attend the first Clayton Antique Boat Show on the banks of the St Lawrence River. Meanwhile, the 1936 Herreshoff ketch *Ticonderoga* sets a new record in the Transpacific race, and Dick Carter's lightweight racer *Rabbit* wins the Fastnet.

1966 Francis Chichester sails around the world solo in *Gypsy Moth IV*.

1970 The controversial IOR rule is created.

1973 The first Opera House Cup regatta is held off Nantuckett Island, USA.

1974 Classic boat aficionados gather in the British Virgin Islands for the first of Foxy's Wooden Boat Regatta.

1974 The first (fibreglass) *Cornish Crabber* is launched in the UK.

1974 *Unicorn*, the first "modern classic" design by Bruce King, is launched in Maine, USA.

1974 Jon Wilson and friends launch *The Wooden Boat* (later plain old *WoodenBoat*) magazine in the United States.

1977 Some 100 boats attend the first Port Townsend Regatta in Washington State, USA.

1980 The first Pors Beac'h festival is held in Britanny, France.

1981 Bernard Cadoret and friends launch *Chasse Marée* magazine in France.

1981 Jean Lorain and Dick Jayson race around La Nioulargue buoy off St Tropez, France, and sow the seeds for the most prestigious classic yacht regatta in the world.

1982 The Associazione Italiana Vele d'Epoca is founded in Italy.

1983 The J-Class yacht *Velsheda* is dragged off her mud berth and sets sail once more off the south coast of Britain.

1984 The town of Risør, on Norway's southern riviera, hosts its first Wooden Boat Festival.

1986 *Chasse Marée* launches the first of its cult festivals in Douarnenez, France.

1987 Pete Greenfield and friends launch *Classic Boat* magazine in the UK.

1989 American media heiress Elizabeth Meyer restores the J-Class yacht *Endeavour* at the Royal Huisman yard in Holland. The first Australian wooden boat festival is held at Goolwa near Adelaide.

1990 Duncan Walker and friends set up Fairlie Restorations on the Hamble, UK.

1992 *Chasse Marée* creates a maritime phenomenon when one and a half million people and 2200 boats gather for the first Brest festival in France.

1992 The America's Cup prepares for the 21st century by replacing the by now outdated 12-Metres with its own high-tech racing class.

1995 A fatal collision between the Herreshoff schooner *Mariette* and the 6-Metre *Taos Brett* closes down the La Nioulargue regatta.

1995 Kiwi sailors wake up to the call by creating the New Zealand Classic Yacht Association (NZCYA).

1996 The Brest festival scales new peaks when 4 million people and 2500 boats gather to celebrate Europe's maritime "patrimoinage". The Classic Yacht Association of Australia is founded.

1998 Alastair and Fiona Houston hold their first Fife jamboree on the Clyde. French sailing legend Eric Tabarly drowns on his way to Scotland.

1999 Italian fashion house Prada sponsors the Mediterranean classic regatta series under the aegis of the Comité International de la Méditerranée (CIM).

2000 The NZCYA makes the most of the America's Cup circus coming to New Zealand by laying on a week-long classic yacht regatta.

2001 The "greatest yachting regatta ever" comes to Cowes to celebrate the 150th anniversary of the America's Cup – including 37 "Twelves" and five Cup winners.

index

This is a direct referral index with the exception of boatyards and boatbuilders all of which are listed under boatyards. Numbers in *italics* refer to captions.